Teachers as Technology Leaders

A Guide to ISTE Technology Facilitation and Technology Leadership Accreditation

Cordelia R. Twomey

Christopher Shamburg

Laura B. Zieger

International Society for Technology in Education
EUGENE, OREGON • WASHINGTON, DC

Teachers as Technology Leaders

A Guide to ISTE Technology Facilitation
and Technology Leadership Accreditation

Cordelia R. Twomey, Christopher Shamburg, Laura B. Zieger

DIRECTOR OF PUBLISHING
Jean Marie Hall

ACQUISITIONS EDITOR
Scott Harter

PRODUCTION EDITOR
Lynda J. Gansel

PRODUCTION COORDINATOR
Maddelyn High

RIGHTS AND PERMISSIONS ADMINISTRATOR
Diane Durrett

COPY EDITOR
Mary Snyder

COVER DESIGN
Signe Landin

BOOK DESIGN AND LAYOUT
Kim McGovern

International Society for Technology in Education (ISTE)
Washington, DC, Office:
1710 Rhode Island Ave. NW, Suite 900, Washington, DC 20036

Eugene, Oregon, Office:
175 West Broadway, Suite 300, Eugene, OR 97401-3003

Order Desk: 1.800.336.5191
Order Fax: 1.541.302.3778
Customer Service: orders@iste.org
Book Publishing: books@iste.org
Rights and Permissions: permissions@iste.org
Web site: www.iste.org

First Edition
ISBN 10: 1-56484-226-6
ISBN 13: 978-1-56484-226-8

About ISTE

The International Society for Technology in Education (ISTE) is a nonprofit professional organization with a worldwide membership of leaders in education technology. We are dedicated to promoting appropriate uses of technology to support and improve learning, teaching, and administration in PK–12 and teacher education. As part of that mission, ISTE provides high-quality and timely information, services, and materials, such as this book.

ISTE Book Publishing works with experienced educators to develop and produce practical resources for classroom teachers, teacher educators, and technology leaders. Every manuscript we select for publication is carefully peer-reviewed and professionally edited. We look for content that emphasizes the effective use of technology where it can make a difference—increasing the productivity of teachers and administrators; helping students with unique learning styles, abilities, or backgrounds; collecting and using data for decision making at the school and district level; and creating dynamic, project-based learning environments that engage 21st-century learners. We value your feedback on this book and other ISTE products. E-mail us at **books@iste.org**.

ISTE is home of the National Educational Technology Standards (NETS) Project, the National Educational Computing Conference (NECC), and the National Center for Preparing Tomorrow's Teachers to Use Technology (NCPT3). To find out more about these and other ISTE initiatives and to view our complete book list or request a print catalog, visit our Web site at **www.iste.org**. You'll find information about:

- ISTE, our mission, and our members

- Membership opportunities and services

- Online communities and special interest groups (SIGs)

- Professional development services

- Research and evaluation services

- Educator resources

- ISTE's National Technology Standards for Students, Teachers, and Administrators

- *Learning & Leading with Technology* magazine

- *Journal of Research on Technology in Education*

About the Authors

Cordelia Twomey, Ph.D., is a Professor and Chairperson of the Educational Technology Department at New Jersey City University and has her Ph.D. in Educational Technology and her M.A. in Curriculum Development from New York University. She serves as the Teacher Education Editor for the *Journal of Instructional Delivery Systems*. In addition to publishing numerous articles, she is the author of *TechPro: The Information Processing Simulation*, along with Dr. Gertrude Abramson. Her areas of research interest include assistive technology, career education, and international educational technology. Dr. Twomey was part of an educational exchange with the People's Republic of China and has recently returned from an International Studies Grant, looking at technology education in the UK and Ireland.

Christopher Shamburg, Ed.D., is an Assistant Professor in the Educational Technology Department at New Jersey City University and has his doctorate in Instructional Media and Technology from Teachers College Columbia University. Before teaching at NJCU he taught high school English at the Hudson County School of Technology for ten years, where he earned five national and statewide awards for his teaching—Teacher of the Year, the Governor's Teacher Recognition Award, a Geraldine R. Dodge Award for Teacher of Humanities, and two fellowships from the National Endowment for the Humanities. Dr. Shamburg has worked as a consultant for numerous organizations, including the New York City Board of Education, the Institute for Learning Technologies at Columbia University, and the Folger Shakespeare Library. He is the author of numerous articles on educational technology and has presented at over 200 workshops.

Laura Zieger, Ed.D., is an Assistant Professor in the Educational Technology Department and Coordinator of the Discovery Education partnership program at New Jersey City University. Dr. Zieger has her doctorate in Educational Technology from Pepperdine University. Both her MA and BA were earned in English Language and Literature. She serves as a judge for the Software Information Industry Association's CODIE Awards. In addition, she is a reviewer for the *Journal of Interactive Online Learning*, an English and Language Arts Mentor for the teachade online community, and a consultant with Athena Learning Group. Dr. Zieger has presented at numerous international, national, and local conferences and has published numerous articles on the subject of educational technology, teacher education, and school library media.

Contents

Introduction

One of the most important positions in a school today is the teacher as technology leader, the individual who helps students, teachers, and administrators integrate technology into effective classroom learning. These professionals understand a range of hardware and software; help teachers create meaningful curriculum with technology; plan and implement professional development; and lead schools and districts on the safe, ethical, and legal uses of technology.

The depth and variety of these responsibilities require a deep and broad preparation. The International Society for Technology in Education (ISTE) developed the Technology Facilitation and the Technology Leadership Standards for exactly this reason. These standards comprise a well-researched and defined set of knowledge, skills, and dispositions designed to meet the needs of today's learning environments.

With a standards-based preparation, candidates can bring a full toolbox of knowledge, skills, and dispositions to any school or district. They can have different titles such as Technology Coordinator or Technology Integration Specialist or they can be classroom teachers with an expertise and desire to help other teachers integrate technology. When you take these different positions and combine them with the varieties of school sizes, student demographics, geographic locations, and school budgets, the number of possible work situations grows exponentially. With these various circumstances come a variety of needs and roles for the technology expert. An education based on the Technology Facilitation or the Technology Leadership standards gives a graduate the broad knowledge to address the specific characteristics and needs of a school or district. Whether working in a small rural elementary school in the Midwest or a large suburban high school in the South, a candidate's preparation is based on the theory and practice of thousands of experts in the field.

For college and university programs that prepare these candidates, adherence to these standards is proven through accreditation. A program accredited by ISTE prepares your graduates and enhances the practices and professionalism of your faculty. Today accreditation for ISTE and for teacher preparation in general is inextricably tied to assessment. Rather than focusing on auditing the performance of candidates, ISTE accreditation focuses on improving the performance of candidates and programs through the analysis of data and feedback. ISTE accreditation is a collaborative and reflective process that involves an examination and revision of assessments, practices, and values.

Teachers as Technology Leaders provides the context of ISTE Technology Facilitation and Technology Leadership accreditation and the procedures and habits to develop and maintain an ISTE-accredited program. Just as technology positions are one of the most important in schools, preparing effective candidates is one of the most important responsibilities for colleges and universities.

This book is designed to assist educators who are involved in programs that prepare candidates to become technology leaders.

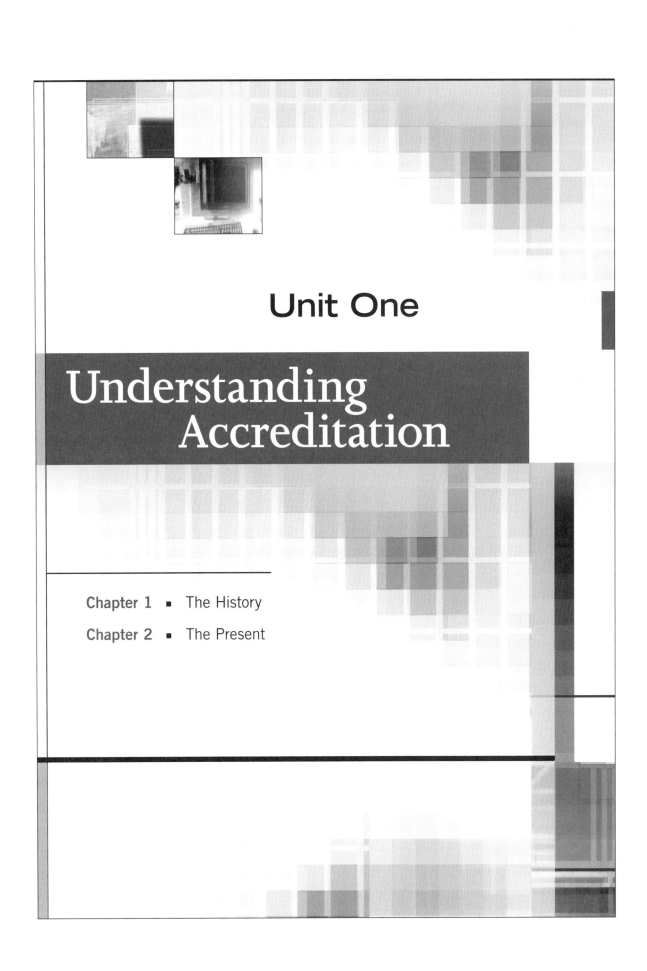

Unit One

Understanding Accreditation

chapter one

The History

 The typical college student has changed dramatically over the centuries. For example, in the late 1800s, college was viewed as a place for the wealthy… or the extremely fortunate. At the end of World War II, with the G.I. Bill of Rights, veterans comprised almost half of the country's total collegiate enrollment. After the G.I. Bill, there was more of a focus on access, skills, and merit-based admissions and grades. With the Civil Rights movement, Open Enrollment changed college from a dream to a reality for many. Yet accreditation has remained a constant part of the college landscape for over 200 years. Regardless of the demographics of the student population, quality education is sought by all.

NCATE

The history of National Council for the Accreditation of Teacher Education (NCATE) accreditation can be traced back to the normal schools themselves and the American Association for Teacher Education, a pre-cursor of the American Association of Colleges for Teacher Education (AACTE). Teacher educators generated their own standards and applied them—creating directories of accredited and unaccredited programs. After several years of negotiation with AACTE, the National Council for Accreditation of Teacher Education was established in the mid 1950s. It was based in large measure on a principle of parity among AACTE and National Education Association (NEA) members (Raths, 2000).

Founded in 1954, NCATE is a nonprofit, nongovernmental alliance of 33 national professional education and public organizations representing millions of Americans who support high-quality teacher preparation programs. A sampling of members includes the American Association of Colleges for Teacher Education, American Library Association, Association for Supervision and Curriculum Development, Council for Exceptional Children, International Society for Technology in Education, National Association of State Boards of Education, National Education Association, National Council for the Social Studies, and National Science Teachers Association.

NCATE accredits a large number of teacher education programs at colleges and universities in the United States. Through a carefully constructed set of outcome-based criteria, NCATE accreditation attests to programmatic quality. This seal of excellence gives colleges and universities important "bragging rights" that attract applicants and recognition of excellence. School districts prefer hiring teachers from NCATE-accredited colleges. Recognition of the acknowledged quality of NCATE-accredited institutions also allows reciprocity so that teachers can practice their skills in states other than where they received their credentials.

The professional associations that comprise NCATE appoint representatives to NCATE's boards who are qualified by education and experience in their fields. All governing board members are trained by the agency on its standards, policies, and procedures, including the processes for revision and establishment of policies, and the policies for making accreditation decisions; decisions on state partnership applications, and decisions on applications for the recognition of program standards. The professional associations that comprise NCATE also provide financial support and participate in the development of NCATE standards, policies, and procedures.

Different entities are accredited by NCATE, and will hereafter be referred to as "the Unit." In many cases the Unit is the College of Education, the School of Education, or the Division of Education. The Unit often contains several different departments or majors, all of which take some responsibility in preparing students to become teachers. Each department within the Unit has its own Specialized Professional Association (SPA). One of the SPAs that governs departments of Educational Technology is the International Society for Technology in Education (ISTE). Since 1990, ISTE has been the professional education organization responsible for recommending guidelines for accreditation to NCATE for programs in educational computing and technology teacher preparation.

Under a division of work, NCATE reviews the pedagogical aspects of educational technology programs while ISTE reviews the content knowledge and skills of students in such programs. The former involves the visit of a team of professionals for discussions with faculty and students and review of documents. In contrast, the review of specific educational technology content does not require such visits. What such a review does require is a document demonstrating that a program meets ISTE standards—the eight thematic standards for a technology facilitator or leader. Officers of ISTE in charge of the reviews investigate educational technology departments, which demonstrate their candidates' mastery of the standards through items taught in their courses.

ISTE

ISTE was formed in 1989 when the International Council for Computers in Education (ICCE) merged with the International Association for Computing in Education (IACE). In 2002, ISTE merged with the National Educational Computing Association (NECA), the supporting nonprofit organization behind the National Educational Computing Conference (NECC), which has been held annually since 1979.

ISTE's Accreditation and Standards Committee established—and regularly updates—guidelines for evaluating university educational computing and technology programs in the United States. In 1996 and 1997, NCATE approved ISTE's performance-based foundation standards for all teacher preparation programs, as well as approving specific requirements for special endorsements and degrees such as the Educational Computing and Technology Leadership Advanced Program. Institutions offering this program should respond to the corresponding set of program standards. "Endorsement" indicates that these programs prepare teachers for an add-on endorsement to an existing teaching certificate.

New guidelines for the Educational Computing and Technology Facilitation and Leadership Programs were approved by NCATE in February 2002 and have been released in the NCATE Approved Curriculum Guide document.

The NETS (National Educational Technology Standards) project, which is an initiative of ISTE's Accreditation and Professional Standards Committee, has as its primary goal "to enable stakeholders in P–12 education to develop national standards for the educational uses of technology that facilitate school improvement in the United States" (ISTE, 2002). The outcomes are the NETS•S (students), NETS•T (teachers), and the NETS•A (administrators), all of which directly or indirectly correspond to the Technology Facilitation (TF) and the Technology Leadership (TL) standards. Table 1 illustrates the milestones of the NETS movement.

TABLE 1 ■ Milestones in the evolution of NETS.

NETS MILESTONES

1989
ISTE Accreditation and Standards Committee (ASC) begins work on teacher standards.

1990
ISTE becomes a constituent member of the National Council for the Accreditation of Teacher Education (NCATE).

1993
ISTE publishes Technology Foundation Standards for All Teachers with 13 performance indicators.

1994
ISTE pilots first student standards development in the Teachers, Technology and Children Online Standards (TTACOS) project in Florida, Texas, and California.

Teachers as Technology Leaders

NETS MILESTONES *(Continued)*

1996

NASA funds first partnership meetings to establish national technology standards for students.

ISTE Standards Partnership holds planning meeting on September 23–24 and names the standards the National Educational Technology Standards (NETS).

1997

U.S. OERI's Star Schools initiative funds writing/reviewing team meetings.

ISTE publishes revised Technology Foundation Standards for All Teachers with 18 performance indicators.

1998

With funding from the Milken Family Foundation, ISTE publishes a first draft of technology standards for students and resources to support them.

NETS for Students (NETS•S) booklet is introduced at NECC 1998.

1999

Learning & Leading with Technology begins correlating article contents to NETS.

With U.S. Department of Education OERI's Star Schools Leadership and NETS Partnership funds, ISTE publishes *NETS for Students—Connecting Curriculum and Technology*. (OERI distributes 20,000 free copies, and ISTE distributes 20,000 free copies.)

2000

With funding from the U.S. Department of Education PT^3 grant and NETS Partners, NETS for Teachers (NETS•T) are reviewed and revised.

ISTE releases NETS•T at NECC 2000 (23 performance indicators).

2001

With PT^3 funding, NETS Assessment Writing Meetings are held.

Technology Standards for School Administrators (TSSA) Consortium asks ISTE to manage the TSSA Project; TSSA standards released November 2001.

2002

With support from consortium partners, the U.S. Department of Education and PBS TeacherLine, ISTE publishes *NETS•T—Preparing Teachers to Use Technology*.

ISTE adopts the TSSA as NETS for Administrators (NETS•A).

With funding from the U.S. Department of Education PT^3 project, ISTE publishes NETS•A poster.

ISTE publishes *Making Technology Standards Work for You—A Guide for School Administrators*.

2003

With PT^3 and partnership funding, ISTE publishes *NETS•T—Resources for Assessment*.

(Roblyer, 2003)

The National Educational Technology Standards

NETS for Students (NETS•S)

The NETS•S were originally published in 1998 and represent the first publication of the NETS project. They "synthesized responses to proposed educational technology standards from many groups and individuals across the nation who participated in conference sessions, technology forum meetings, Internet dialogue, and surveys" (ISTE, 2000). The same framework of six standards—plus two additional standards—outline the TF and the TL programs standards. The additional two categories in the TF and the TL standards focus on "Procedures, Policies, Planning, and Budgeting for Technology Environments" and "Leadership and Vision."

The book, *The National Educational Technology Standards for Students: Connecting Curriculum and Technology* (ISTE, 2000), provides lesson plans that give examples of the use of technology to support content learning as well as multidisciplinary resource units, workshop staging guides, NETS project partnerships, and other resources.

The No Child Left Behind (NCLB) Act suggests that standards will be a primary component of educational accountability for years to come. Technology standards constitute part of the requirements of NCLB. As a result, many states are working to integrate the NETS for Students into their own curriculum standards.

In Chapters 5 and 6 you will see how the TF and the TL standards are correlated to the NETS•S.

NETS for Teachers (NETS•T)

The NETS•T focus on pre-service teacher education by defining "the fundamental concepts, knowledge, skills, and attitudes for applying technology in educational settings" and providing "a framework for implementing technology in teaching and learning that has been widely used in universities, state departments of education, and school districts across the nation" (ISTE, 2002). Just like NETS•S, the same framework of six standards—plus two additional standards—outline the TF and the TL program standards. The additional two categories in the TF and the TL standards focus on "Procedures, Policies, Planning, and Budgeting for Technology Environments" and "Leadership and Vision."

The book, *The National Educational Technology Standards for Teachers: Preparing Teachers to Use Technology* (ISTE, 2002), provides teachers with ways to integrate technology into their professional preparation and into their classroom by providing a myriad of subject-related resources.

NETS for Administrators (NETS•A)

The NETS•A follows on the success of the NETS•S and the NETS•T and is built upon the work of the Consortium for Technology Standards for School Administrators (TSSA). ISTE participated in the TSSA Collaborative and had a lead role in managing the inclusive, broad-based development process.

In January 2001, administrators from across the country came together to develop the initial draft of the Technology Standards for School Administrators (TSSA). The NETS•A were adopted in January 2002. The standards represent a national consensus among educational stakeholders of what best indicates effective school leadership for comprehensive and appropriate use of technology in schools.

TABLE 2 ■ NETS overview.

NETS	STANDARDS CATEGORIES
NETS for Students (NETS•S) Six standards categories, 14 indicators, along with profiles of performance indicators for each grade level	1. Basic Operations and Concepts 2. Social, Ethical, and Human Issues 3. Technology Productivity Tools 4. Technology Communications Tools 5. Technology Research Tools 6. Technology Problem-Solving and Decision-Making Tools
NETS for Teachers (NETS•T) Six standards categories, 23 indicators, along with profiles of performance indicators for general, professional, and student teaching/internship performance levels	I. Technology Operations and Concepts II. Planning and Designing Learning Environments and Experiences III. Teaching, Learning, and the Curriculum IV. Assessment and Evaluation V. Productivity and Professional Tools VI. Social, Ethical, Legal, and Human Issues
NETS for Administrators (NETS•A) Six standards categories, 31 indicators, along with profiles of performance indicators for principals, district program directors, and superintendents	I. Leadership and Vision II. Learning and Teaching III. Productivity and Professional Practice IV. Support, Management, and Operations V. Assessment and Evaluation VI. Social, Legal, and Ethical Issues

The NETS Project was established in order to set the standards for educational uses of technology that would facilitate school improvement. These standards have influenced program accreditation, state curriculum, and certification requirements across the country.

Technology Facilitation (TF)

The International Society for Technology in Education recognizes that educational computing and technology foundations are essential for all teachers. ISTE also acknowledges educational computing and technology specialty areas beyond these foundations and has established program standards for initial and advanced programs. These program standards will assist teacher education units as well as professional organizations and agencies in understanding and evaluating the educational preparation needed for specialization within the field.

Technology Facilitation Endorsement: Technology Facilitation endorsement programs that meet ISTE standards prepare candidates to serve as building/campus-level technology facilitators. Candidates completing this program will exhibit knowledge, skills, and dispositions equipping them to teach technology applications; demonstrate effective use of technology to support student learning of content; and provide professional development, mentoring, and basic technical assistance for other teachers who require support in their efforts to apply technology to support student learning (ISTE, 2002).

Technology Leadership (TL)

Technology leadership candidates demonstrate that they have met the Technology Facilitation Standards prior to full admission to the Technology Leadership Program.

The TL program standards are aligned with the six National Educational Technology Standards for Teachers but extend the performance expectations of each standard. These increased expectations reflect preparation for serving as a director, coordinator, or technology integration specialist at the district, regional, and/or state levels, assisting teachers as well as technology facilitators in their efforts to support student learning and educator professional growth with technology (ISTE, 2002).

Technology Leadership (TL)—Advanced Program: Technology Leadership advanced programs that meet ISTE standards prepare candidates to serve as technology directors, coordinators, or specialists. Special preparation in computing systems, facilities planning and management, instructional program development, staff development, and other advanced applications of technology to support student learning and assessment will prepare candidates to serve in technology-related leadership positions at district, regional, and/or state levels (Revised—Fall 2001) (ISTE, 2002).

Summary

The first chapter provided an overview of the history of accreditation and insight into NCATE and ISTE, whose NETS•S, NETS•T, NETS•A, TF, and TL standards have become the benchmarks for technology integration. The next chapter will focus on the evolving role of the technology facilitator and the technology leader from the state, college, and P–12 perspectives.

chapter two

The Present

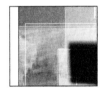

The focus of Chapter 2 is to look at the evolving role of the technology facilitators and leaders from state, teacher preparation program, and P–12 student perspectives. The state perspective will examine states that use TF and TL standards as accrediting and licensing devices, as well as initiatives that come from the state to the school districts regarding teachers and technology integration. The second section will look at the challenges facing colleges in the preparation of technology facilitators and leaders. The impact of effectively delivered technology on student learning will be covered in the third section of this chapter. Yet, in actuality, these three categories are not separate topics—they are all intertwined, as you will soon see. States, accrediting agencies, colleges, and classroom teachers are directly connected, with technology being the common thread that links them.

From a State Perspective

NCATE has partnerships with 50 states, including the District of Columbia and Puerto Rico. In 17 partnership states, all public teacher education institutions are NCATE accredited. In 28 partnership states, a majority of all the teacher education institutions are NCATE accredited.

Twenty-five states have adopted or adapted NCATE unit standards as their own and apply them to all institutions for purposes of state approval. They rely on NCATE's program review process in lieu of their own for purposes of NCATE accreditation and state approval. NCATE standards are closely aligned with state teacher education standards due—in large part—to the relationship between NCATE and its partner states.

The NCATE State Relations group provides significant professional development and training to state staff who administer the state partnership program. These services include the annual State Partnership Clinic, which helps state staff improve their understanding of systems for teacher education accountability. In addition, the majority of NCATE teacher education staff from partner states participate in NCATE Board of Examiner (BOE) training at no charge to the states. Those who serve on the NCATE BOE have the opportunity to visit other states and institutions and observe a broad range of different systems for assuring quality teacher education—at NCATE's expense. These experiences are useful to their work at the state level in assuring teacher education accountability. Lastly, NCATE provides state-based training sessions designed to prepare reviewers to evaluate teacher education institutions in the state.

Technology positions are rapidly becoming certification- or license-bearing in many states across the country. That, coupled with the growing needs of school districts to support teachers in the effective use of technology, makes obvious the need for TF and TL higher education programs. Therefore, those programs that are part of their institution's NCATE process will need to meet the requirements developed in accordance with ISTE's TF and TL standards.

NCATE has adopted ISTE's guidelines for use in the accreditation of technology facilitators, technology leaders, and secondary computer science teachers. Teacher preparation entities seeking accreditation for any of these programs develop a program report addressing the performance-based standards identified for the appropriate program. New guidelines for the Educational Computing and Technology Facilitation and Leadership Programs were approved by NCATE in February 2002 and have been released in the NCATE Approved Curriculum Guide document.

There are technology standards that have been developed and adopted nationally, as well as on a state-by-state basis. As stated earlier, ISTE began the process with the NETS•S; then NETS•T formed the basis for standards for teachers. Many states have adopted, adapted, aligned, or referenced NETS in developing their own state technology standards for students and teachers. In the next section, we will look at the link between the TF standards, the TL standards, and institutions of higher education.

From a College/University Perspective

As school districts continue to allocate more and more dollars to purchase technology, the need for qualified people to make those systems run smoothly grows accordingly. Along with a technology financial budget is the need for a significant investment in educator preparation to ensure that these new technologies are being used effectively in the classroom. How are districts encouraging their teachers to be not only pioneers but also leaders in technology education? Many school districts employ Technology Facilitators to help solve this problem. The technology facilitator or technology leader is the person who blazes a trail for technology in the school or district and who understands how all the hardware, software, policies, and procedures fit together in the big picture of the school's or the district's technology implementation plan (Bailey & Frazier, 2004).

There are many graduate education programs in the United States that attempt to address these needs. However, there are theoretical differences from program to program, and these differences impact a candidate's future career goals. Those programs that adhere to ISTE's TF and TL standards are delivering a curriculum that ensures that the candidate will be qualified to be a technology facilitator or leader anywhere. This may include examining the underlying functionality of software and hardware and carefully aligning technology with educational objectives and learning theories like constructivism, collaborative and cooperative learning, and project-based learning.

Candidates who select the Technology Facilitation field study the design, development, and management of instructional materials through the use of educational technologies. Their primary role is to be a technology integration specialist—one who helps teachers integrate technology at the classroom level and manages professional development for schools. The *school* is their domain.

Since 2001, several states including Louisiana, North Carolina, Illinois, and Pennsylvania have approved teacher certification endorsements for Technology Facilitator certification. The criteria for the certification of these technology experts include such requirements as a teaching certificate and between 9 and 18 semester hours of graduate credit in educational technology courses relevant to the ISTE Educational Computing and Technology Standards for Technology Facilitators. Although some states still have not approved Technology Facilitator certification endorsements, there exist many programs intended for the preparation of Technology Facilitators. Over 40 institutions in the Mid-Atlantic region alone offer such programs (Miller, Snelbeck, Teitelbaum, & Cooper, 2002).

Candidates who select the Technology Leadership field of study are expected to be experts in planning, implementation, and assessment, not only of leading technologies, but also in learning theory as it integrates with technology. They are able to evaluate any technology and design effective learning in any content, at any grade level. The *district* is their domain.

Bailey and Frazier (2004) offer some generally accepted ideas about what districts are looking for in applicants for technology leadership positions. The district technology leader is to plan, develop, implement, evaluate, and maintain an exemplary first-class technology program for the district. This will include support for students, teachers, support staff, and administrative staff. These requirements—and more—are the standards by which ISTE measures Technology Leadership programs in colleges of education.

Let's look at some examples. Candidates at National-Louis University who enter the program with an Illinois teaching certification can receive certification as a P–12 Technology Specialist upon completing the required courses and receiving passing scores on several teaching exams. The program is held on-campus in computer labs with no more than 15 candidates per class. Upon completion, candidates are expected to:

1. Use and model research-based best practices in the integration of technology in the P–12 curriculum.

2. Mentor and provide technical assistance to P–12 teachers in their planning for, implementation of, and assessment of student-centered engaged learning environments that make effective use of technology. Such student-centered learning environments will address the diverse needs (cognitive, physical, social, and emotional) of students while meeting local, state, and national standards.

3. Practice collaborative inquiry as students and professionals; assessing, reflecting, and taking action to improve the use of technology in the P–12 learning environment and the infrastructure to support that use; promoting equitable access to current technologies, and addressing social, ethical, legal, and human issues surrounding the use of technology in P–12 schools.

4. Increase their roles as professionals in the area of educational technology, participating in professional associations and professional development activities in their school setting. (http://myclass.nl.edu/tie/philosophy.htm)

The fully online, ISTE-accredited TF program at New Jersey City University leading to the Master of Arts degree in Educational Technology is designed to meet the needs of classroom teachers who want to apply technology to the learning process and for individuals wishing to develop leadership skills as site-based technology coordinators. The Master's Degree in Educational Technology is intended to develop a broad range of technological expertise, while at the same time focusing clearly on the new way that technology is changing how students and educators create and understand knowledge. Participants in the program learn the new role of information, not as isolated facts, but as building blocks to develop cognitive skills.

These and many other programs have met the standards outlined by ISTE, regardless of their state's certification requirements. They are meeting the need for distinct instructional specialists to support teachers as technology facilitators and leaders in the effective use of technology.

From a P–12 Perspective

The need for school personnel dedicated to leading and facilitating technology integration in P–12 schools became apparent in the early 1990s when computers were making their way out of computer labs and into other classrooms. Until the early 1990s many schools housed their computers in a single lab that was usually the responsibility of a computer teacher who taught programming, DOS, and perhaps a few packaged programs. The computer teacher was similar to a chemistry teacher who has the responsibility of managing lab equipment and chemicals. He or she would load software, replace keyboards, and keep the lab in working order. There was little emphasis on curriculum integration because the curriculum was computer skills. The computer teacher's monopoly on the school's PCs started to dissolve around the time of the extinction of the 5¼ floppy disk and the dot matrix printer. During the mid 1990s computers started to become a part of third-grade classrooms, high school English courses, and seventh-grade social studies curriculums. Thus, with the inclusion of technology in the classrooms arose the need for a new type of school personnel, dedicated to the successful integration of technology in schools.

Today, P–12 teachers and administrators have the potential and the responsibility to integrate technology into their curriculum. As ISTE developed its NETS•S and NETS•T, a need arose for a superseding set of standards for those responsible for directly supporting teachers as they integrate technology:

The Technology Facilitator (TF) program standards are aligned with the six National Educational Technology Standards for Teachers, but extend the performance expectations of each candidate to reflect preparation for serving as mentor, coordinator, or technology integration specialist, assisting the teachers in their efforts to support student learning and professional growth with technology (ISTE, n.d.).

The Technology Leadership (TL) program standards are aligned with the six National Educational Technology Standards for Teachers, but extend the performance expectations of each standard to reflect preparation for serving as a director, coordinator, or technology integration specialist at the district, regional, and/or state levels, assisting teachers as well as Technology Facilitators in their efforts to support student learning and educator professional growth with technology (ISTE, 2005).

The TF and the TL standards extend the NETS•T standards by enhancing the responsibilities in substance and detail. Technology facilitators and leaders have a spectrum of responsibilities in P–12 schools. Just consider the variety of school sizes; the geographic, demographic, and legislative differences among states; the varying resources within schools; and the spectrum of goals and pedagogies from kindergarten to high school. Now also consider the myriad of technology issues that affect districts and classrooms—troubleshooting hardware, learning new software, evaluating resources, developing curriculum, funding equipment purchases, and effectively assessing students... to name a few. A candidate who successfully completes a program accredited for Technology Facilitator will be ready to do this.

Though there are many school personnel involved in technology, Technology Facilitators and Leaders work as ambassadors among policy, technology and pedagogy. Practically every national organization and state department of education embeds technology in its standards, and every teacher should be actively involved in technology integration. Many schools employ Web masters, lab managers, IT directors, hardware maintenance personnel, and technicians. The TF and TL standards prepare people to coordinate efforts with these technical personnel, administrators, and the classroom teachers. The spectrum of responsibilities is captured by this job description for a Site Technology Coordinator posted by the Vail School District (2002) in Arizona.

JOB TITLE: *Site Technology Coordinator*

Summary: Responsible for the planning, implementation, and use of technology in the assigned school.

Essential Duties and Responsibilities include the following. Other duties may be assigned.

- Coordinate efforts with other Site Technology Coordinators and District Director of Technology.

- Provide leadership in technology curriculum.

- Provide hardware and software instruction to staff.

- Provide staff development on technology.

- Assist in supervising Computer Paraprofessional.

- Supervise and coordinate services available through the Local Area Network (LAN) and the Wide Area Network (WAN).

- Coordinate the use of technology by teachers, administrators, support staff, and students.

- Review, evaluate, and inform instructional staff of recent technology developments in commercial products.

- Coordinate the purchase of technology equipment and materials.

- Maintain an inventory of technology equipment and materials.

- Develop and provide training for teachers, administrators, and staff.

- Explore options for grant proposals designed to secure additional funding for the district in the area of technology and share results with Principal and Director of Technology.

- Coordinate the set-up and maintenance of equipment and networks.

- Manage the CLIP program at the assigned school.

The posting goes on to describe the physical demands of the job that include, "The employee frequently is required to climb various equipment including but not limited to ladders and step stools or balance and stoop, kneel, crouch, and crawl. The employee must regularly lift and/or move up to 50 pounds. Specific vision abilities required by this job include close vision, peripheral vision, and ability to adjust focus" (Vail School District, 2002).

The expectations illustrated in this posting, coupled with the importance of educational technology in the learning process, necessitates a well-researched and defined set of standards for the preparation of technology facilitators and leaders. The knowledge, skills, and dispositions of the TF and TL standards address the broad and varied roles needed in schools and school districts.

The following three vignettes illustrate the spectrum of responsibilities for which TF and TL programs prepare candidates. Although Vignette One is more aligned with the expectations of a technology facilitator program, and Vignette Three with a technology leader, you can see a continuum of skills running throughout all of the stories.

In each of these cases, exemplary technology professionals worked toward the ultimate goal of improving student learning with technology. Staff development, legal and ethical issues, improving student learning, and learning and teaching new technologies are all in the domain of the TF and the TL standards.

Vignette One: Integration

Sarah is a technology coordinator in an elementary school in a rural area. She helps all of her teachers integrate technology into their lessons. Some come to her monthly workshops on topics of interest and others ask for specific help. She works with these teachers after school and makes appointments to come into their classes during the school day.

Her recent work with one teacher illustrates some of the important aspects of the job of Technology Facilitator. Mrs. Gibbons, a fourth-grade teacher, is an early adapter of technology. For years she had her students create PowerPoint presentations on the history of the state. They would integrate images and information from the Web with their own collection of images and first-person narratives from neighbors and family members. Students would use digital photography, digital audio recorders and create a presentation on particular aspects of their state's history. A few months before starting this semester's project, Mrs. Gibbons had an idea to use digital video editing instead of a PowerPoint presentation. She had limited knowledge of what this would involve, so she asked Sarah about the feasibility of this project. Though Sarah had some experience, she researched the hardware and software options, discussed these with Mrs. Gibbons and the building principal, and budgeted enough for an inexpensive but useful set of tools.

Sarah created a quick-start guide for the students, gave Mrs. Gibbons an overview, and taught a lesson to the students on the technical procedures of shooting and editing. Next, she and Mrs. Gibbons created a lesson on the legal and ethical uses of digital material. They discovered that two students had experience with digital video so Sarah and Mrs. Gibbons asked them to serve as tutors for the other students. Finally, using the computer lab during one period a day, during lunch and after school, the students created a variety of short movies that included archival footage from the Web, original video, interviews, images, and music.

Vignette Two: Supporting Student Learning

Jerry is the technology coordinator at a charter high school in an urban area in the Northeast. The school is small and has a unique mission to foster a learning community. While the students benefit from the small class sizes and close-knit community, the school cannot run elective classes because too few students request them.

This year three students wanted the school to offer a French class. Even though their current Spanish teacher is certified to teach French, the school could not afford to run a class for three students. They would have to take Spanish. Ms. Connor, the school principal, asked Jerry to see if there was anything online for the students to use. Jerry found a grant offered by the state to pilot innovative online education programs. He contacted several other small schools and together with their administrators and Technology Facilitators developed a program to offer online elective classes though their consortium. The online elective courses were taught by teachers in the different schools for subjects such as biochemistry, cinema studies, French, and statistics.

This program involved months of planning, collaboration, staff development, and a partnership with a local institution. Jerry is also responsible for administering the grant, writing the quarterly reports, and sending assessments to the state.

Vignette Three: Policy and Procedures

Turner County School District prides itself on its learner-centered approach to education and educational technology. Students are given unstructured time in the labs and libraries to work on independent projects. The school has made a commitment to lending laptops and tablet PCs through their library system, and several of the buildings have wireless Internet access.

Recently, the administration has become aware of students exploiting advanced search techniques of a certain search engine to find and download music illegally. Emilio, the district technology administrator, was called in by the district superintendent to address this problem. Besides stopping the ethical and legal breaches of the students, the superintendent was worried that the school district would be liable for allowing students to illegally download music.

Emilio took proactive measures. Both the software on the computers and the firewall on the district's network were upgraded to prevent the use of peer-to-peer applications commonly used for downloading music free. In addition to fixing this problem immediately, Emilio also reviewed and revised the district's acceptable use policy to make sure this was addressed. Then he designed and conducted several faculty professional development workshops on the legal and ethical issues of copyright and digital technologics and what to look out for when students are using computers.

Summary

Unit I provided the background for understanding the history of accreditation, NCATE, and ISTE, and the place of the TF and the TL standards from the classroom, the college/university, and the state perspectives. Unit II provides practical advice for getting your program through the accreditation process.

Unit Two

Preparing for Accreditation

chapter three

Defining Your Program

A simple explanation of the difference between a Technology Leadership program and a Technology Facilitation program is that a Leadership program advances the standards of a Facilitation program. Though this explanation is helpful, you must look at the deep and powerful philosophical differences that a TF or a TL program has in the context of your institution. As you read this chapter and the rest of the book, you will see Facilitators and Leaders focus on different groups and perform different tasks, albeit all under the general vision of ISTE standards. Does your program or institution prioritize teachers' work in classrooms or the broader work of policy and administration? When correlating your program to the vision of your institution and its conceptual framework, the choice of TF or TL can fundamentally answer the question of who you are.

The ISTE/NCATE standards lie at the heart of quality teacher preparation. ISTE has developed performance assessment standards for initial and advanced educational computing and technology programs including (1) the technology facilitation initial endorsement and (2) the technology leadership advanced program. If an institution offers undergraduate and/or graduate programs in educational technology, it must respond to these program standards.

A TF program can be an individual degree (e.g., an MA in Technology Facilitation) or an endorsement. It should be noted that ISTE considers any program to be "initial" that prepares candidates for the Technology Facilitation endorsement. These programs may be at the graduate or undergraduate level. "Endorsement" indicates that these programs prepare teachers for an add-on endorsement to an existing teaching certificate.

ISTE standards include but are not limited to evidence of meeting prerequisite standards, i.e., NETS for Teachers and verification that the individual holds a basic teaching license (Standard TF-I.). Advanced programs are those programs at the post-baccalaureate level for the advanced education of personnel who have previously completed or are simultaneously completing the Technology Facilitation endorsement. The Technology Leadership program is designed to prepare personnel for a leadership role in educational technology at the district or higher level. ISTE standards include but are not limited to evidence of meeting prerequisite standards, i.e., NETS for Teachers and Technology Facilitation and verification that the individual holds a basic teaching license (Standard TL-I). Please note that licensure requirements vary by state and that this will impact the classification of your program to NCATE as Initial, Advanced, or Other School Personnel. Therefore, your TF or TL program can be initial, advanced or other school personnel in your NCATE and ISTE applications.

In general, Technology Facilitation standards are for those who provide direct support to teachers while Technology Leadership standards are designed for those who have some combination of policymaking, policy implementation, and/or administrative responsibilities.

ISTE Technology Facilitation Standards

This licensure program will prepare candidates to serve as building/campus-level technology facilitators. Candidates completing this program will exhibit knowledge, skills, and dispositions equipping them to teach technology applications; demonstrate effective use of technology to support student learning of content; and provide professional development, mentoring, and basic technical assistance for other teachers who require support in their efforts to apply technology to support student learning.

ISTE Technology Leadership Standards

This licensure program will prepare candidates to serve as technology specialists who are defined at the beginning levels of the Leadership Standards. Special preparation in computing systems, facilities planning, instructional program development, and other advanced applications of technology to support student learning and assessment will prepare candidates to serve in technology-related leadership positions at school and possibly district levels. The TL program standards are aligned with the six National Educational Technology Standards for Teachers (NETS•T), but extend the performance expectations of each standard to reflect preparation for serving as a director, coordinator, or technology integration specialist at the district, regional, and/or state level, assisting teachers as well as Technology Facilitators in their efforts to support student learning and educator professional growth with technology.

Prerequisite Standards—Technology Facilitation Standards: Educational technology leadership candidates demonstrate that they have met the Technology Facilitation Standards prior to full admission to the Technology Leadership Program. (http://cnets.iste.org/ncate/n_fac-stands.html)

Two examples of ways in which the standards differ are:

TECHNOLOGY FACILITATION (TF)	TECHNOLOGY LEADERSHIP (TL)
TF-III: Teaching, Learning, and the Curriculum.	**TL-III: Teaching, Learning, and the Curriculum.**
Educational technology facilitators apply and implement curriculum plans that include methods and strategies for utilizing technology to maximize student learning.	Educational technology leaders model, design, and disseminate curriculum plans that include methods and strategies for applying technology to maximize student learning.
TF-VII: Procedures, Policies, Planning, and Budgeting for Technology Environments.	**TL-VII: Procedures, Policies, Planning, and Budgeting for Technology Environments.**
Educational technology facilitators promote the development and implementation of technology infrastructure, procedures, policies, plans, and budgets for P–12 schools.	Educational technology leaders coordinate development and direct implementation of technology infrastructure procedures, policies, plans, and budgets for P–12 schools.

Organizing the Process

Planning and organizing are two of the most important components for both the ISTE and the NCATE accreditation processes. The focus of Chapter 4 is the administrative component, ensuring that all of the stakeholders understand their roles in the process. Who is a "stakeholder?" A stakeholder is anyone who has a vested interest in seeing your program and your candidates succeed and who can help you meet your goals, as well as those who provide foundational or content knowledge, skills, and dispositions that support TF or TL functions. If your program is designed to create candidates who will be tomorrow's technology facilitators and leaders, you need to lead by example and use all available resources—people, procedures, and technology.

Involving All of the Stakeholders

NCATE distinguishes between initial teacher preparation and advanced preparation programs. Initial teacher preparation is defined by NCATE as "programs at baccalaureate or post-baccalaureate levels that prepare candidates for the first license to teach" (NCATE, 2002). They include four-year baccalaureate, post-baccalaureate, and master's programs leading to licensure. Some initial teacher preparation programs are five-year programs combining undergraduate- and graduate-level work. Others are fifth-year programs for candidates with a baccalaureate in an academic area—fifth-year programs often include year-long internships. Advanced programs are offered at the post-baccalaureate level to (1) licensed teachers continuing their education and (2) candidates preparing to work in schools in roles other than teaching. Advanced programs often lead to master's, specialist, or doctoral degrees, but some are non-degree licensure programs. From our research, we have found that many of the institutions pursuing ISTE TF and TL accreditation have programs that are on the advanced level.

The reason for distinguishing between the programs is that your type of preparation program will determine who the stakeholders are. Stakeholders could include full-time and adjunct faculty who teach on campus, off campus, and online; candidates; alumni administrators (such as representatives from the Graduate office and the Online Learning Department, if you have one); employers of your candidates; the Technology Club; academic computing labs; the library; the IT Department; and all other related departments.

Involve all the stakeholders from the beginning. Start by holding a large meeting in which you invite everyone involved in the process, so that they have an understanding of what is happening. Clearly define roles and responsibilities. Give everyone reading materials on NCATE; your department, its history, and course offerings; and any other background information. Remember—no one person can be an expert in all areas. Call upon other people's expertise to help you through the process.

The Procedures

Establish procedures early on and share them with everyone. For example, you will have much better attendance at meetings if you set a schedule and stick to it. People want to be able to know that the first Monday of the month, from 1:00 to 2:00, is reserved for Committee X and the third Thursday of the month, from 10:00 to 11:00, for Committee Y. Post the schedule on the Web, use listservs to e-mail announcements, and also send hard-copy reminders.

For every meeting that you call or attend, minutes should be created immediately afterward. It is easier to create minutes while the material is still fresh, rather than trying to recreate minutes weeks later. Minutes are a requirement for NCATE and the Unit should have a template that everyone's minutes should follow. In your department meetings be sure to include discussions of the various committee meetings that your faculty attended—such as the Assessment Committee and the Diversity Committee.

Members of your department will invariably be asked to serve on the Unit-wide NCATE committees, which are usually organized around NCATE's six standards:

    I.   Candidate Knowledge, Skills, and Dispositions

    II.   Assessment System and Unit Evaluation

    III.   Field Experiences and Clinical Practice

    IV.   Diversity

    V.   Faculty Qualifications, Performance, Development

    VI.   Unit Governance and Resources

It is important to keep the information flowing in both directions. Bring the information from the NCATE committees to your TF or TL accreditation process and be sure to bring your department's activities to the various Unit-wide NCATE committees. The Unit is going to rely heavily on your program for information on candidate knowledge, skills and dispositions; assessment systems; field experiences and clinical practice; diversity; and your faculty's qualifications, performance, and development—and you need to ensure that the data that you are collecting is in accordance with Unit standards. On the other hand, the NCATE committees will provide you with valuable information that you can utilize from the Unit perspective. You can see the strong interrelationship between your program's TF or TL accreditation process and the Unit's NCATE accreditation process.

Another key piece of advice is, "Prepare, prepare, prepare." If there are people who have been at the institution since your program began, that is an excellent source of history for you. If there had been previous modifications to the program, know what they were and why the changes were made.

Be aware that the NCATE BOE team can review your off-campus and online programs. The questions that they can ask about your off-campus offerings are listed below. This is where having your informed stakeholders will prove helpful.

- What is the institution's commitment to the off-campus programs?

- Why does the institution offer off-campus programs?

- To what degree do the regular campus faculty deliver the programs?

- What are the qualifications of adjunct faculty?

- Is the curriculum an extension of what is offered on-campus, or is it different?

- What are the differences in the delivery of on-and off-campus programs, and are those differences appropriate?

- Are admission requirements the same or different from off-campus programs, and are those differences appropriate?

- How many candidates are enrolled in each off-campus program?

- How are off-campus programs financed and administered?

In addition, the BOE team can pose the following questions about your distance learning courses. Again, having your stakeholders prepared will be beneficial.

- To what extent are the design and delivery of distance learning programs consistent with the mission of the institution and the Unit, supported by a conceptual framework and knowledge base, guided by a long-range plan, and supported by adequate resources?

- Are evaluations of the distance learning programs systematic, ongoing, and used for program improvement? Are evaluation instruments tailored to the unique characteristics and needs of the candidates? How?

- What are the qualifications of faculty members who teach via distance delivery? Are they qualified for their assignments and competent in the methods of delivery?

- To what extent are the balance of part-time and full-time faculty, requirements for scholarship and service, and evaluation processes the same for faculty members who teach via distance learning as for other faculty members?

- What types of technology support are in place for both faculty and candidates, so that technological breakdowns do not interfere with delivery? To what extent are these support systems sufficient and reliable?

- How are distance learning programs, including programs that are acquired through contract with an outside vendor or delivered in a consortium arrangement, controlled, coordinated, and evaluated by the Unit?

- Do distance learning programs in professional education ensure that field experiences and clinical practice are well sequenced, supervised by trained personnel and monitored by Unit faculty, and integrated into the program? Explain.

- Are distance learning candidates provided the same level of advisement and personal access to faculty, monitoring of progress, and assessment as are provided for traditional candidates? In particular, do assessment measures assure that candidates acquire the competencies and objectives established for individual courses?

As an example, we have a totally online program. In preparation for the BOE visit, a group of us met to discuss the above questions. The group included full-time and part-time faculty who teach online and the directors of the Online Learning Department, the Academic Computing Labs, and the Information Technology Department. We all learned from one another and when the BOE team arrived at the university for the NCATE site visit, we were all well informed.

The Technology

In Chapter 7 there is a detailed discussion of using technology for assessment purposes. In this section we will look at ways to make the process more efficient from an administrative standpoint.

- Make sure that the systems the stakeholders are using can communicate.

- Make sure that every stakeholder knows how to use the technology. Plan for training sessions, if necessary.

- Create standardized naming protocols for your documents.

- Make sure that everyone backs up work frequently.

- Create listservs for the various committees and update the lists as needed.

- Everyone's schedule is hectic. We created an online Educational Technology Alumni Association—no dues, no meetings; just the desire to participate in the process.

- For convenience, put surveys online.

- If you have a work study student or a graduate assistant, make sure that his/her technology skills are sufficient to help you process the data.

Look at all available technology—what is available in your department and what also exists in the institution. Work with your IT Department from the beginning of the process, because they might be aware of many resources that you do not know exist.

Setting Timelines

The following timelines are based on an NCATE visit, which is the time when most programs submit their documents for accreditation or re-accreditation. However, your program might need to follow a different schedule. For example, if NCATE just visited your institution but now your new program needs to be accredited to meet your state's accrediting requirements or state licensure mandates, you will follow a different timeline. Check with your institution's NCATE Coordinator for the appropriate dates.

Applying for the TF or TL accreditation process is usually initiated through your Unit's NCATE Coordinator. This person should have the pass codes and Web site address to give to the chief compiler of your report—the point person in your program for the submission of the report.

The deadline for submission of your report (your application for ISTE TF or TL accreditation) is dependent upon the scheduled visit of the NCATE BOE. There is a relatively short timeframe between submission of the report for TF or TL accreditation and the NCATE visit to your school. If your institution is already accredited, the report is to be submitted no more than one semester before the institution's scheduled NCATE visit. If your institution is applying for accreditation for the first time, or if the institution makes a special request, the report is due one year before the NCATE visit. The deadlines for submission are September 15th and February 1st. For example, if your school is expecting a visit in May 2007 and is currently NCATE accredited, you would submit your report one semester before, on September 15th (NCATE, 2006).

The most effective way to set timelines is to work backwards. When is the team coming? If the BOE will be at your institution from May 1–5, work backwards from those dates. However, there are many dates that are important in the cycle, not just the dates of the site visit. During the process your department is expected to provide on-going information to the Unit as well. Institutions with visits in spring 2007 and beyond are expected to meet the expectations listed below, and you will be expected to have information to meet these assessments:

A. Units are expected to have developed and implemented internal performance assessments, which address the following elements:

1. The assessment instruments should be based on professional/state/institutional standards.

2. Assessment instruments and criteria/rubrics should be developed.

3. Assessment instruments and criteria/rubrics should be in use.

4. Data collection should be in process; analysis should have begun.

5. Testing for accuracy, consistency, and fairness should be occurring.

B. Units are expected to have an assessment system in place and operating. The assessment system should address:

1. transition points;

2. major assessments;

3. the design for data collection, analysis, summary, and use;

4. measures that address Unit operations; and

5. description of the use of information technology to maintain the system.

C. Units are expected to have performance data from the following sources:

1. state licensing exams (where applicable);

2. program review reports or state reviews of programs;

3. graduate/employer surveys;

4. assessments of clinical practice; and

5. other key assessments as identified in Unit assessment systems.

Just as assessment changes to meet the evolving needs of students, candidates, and education as a whole, so too does the way that material is submitted. Today, the process requires a fully online submission and has been simplified to focus on eight assessments, which will be discussed in Chapter 7.

Identifying Strengths and Weaknesses in the Current Program

Preparing for ISTE accreditation and the NCATE visit is your opportunity to examine the program objectively and determine what areas need to be revisited. Revision could take the form of adding a course or courses, deleting a course or courses, resequencing courses, or updating courses. If your program was recently created and designed with the TF or the TL standards in mind, there might be little need for course additions or resequencing. If your program was designed several years ago, revisions will probably need to take place.

How will you go about making those changes? What are the steps involved? How long will these modifications take? Remember that with NCATE coming, all of the other departments are going through the same modifications, so the process will proceed much more slowly than usual.

Are you aware of all of the steps? For example, at many institutions there is a required sequence that each new course or program modification must follow: department approval; Dean approval; College of Education Curriculum Committee approval; Vice President approval; and Faculty Senate approval. Start early so that your courses are not bottlenecked in the process because other departments in the Unit will be following the same procedures that you are, to meet their SPA's requirements.

As an example, in reviewing our program, which has five levels of courses, we added a course, updated courses, and resequenced courses. One of the first things that we did was to add a Level II course, Technology Facilitator: Issues and Challenges. This way we are imbedding the TF philosophy early and ensuring that the standards run through all the assignments that the candidate completes.

We also updated courses. For example, Introduction to Hypermedia was upgraded and became Introduction to Authoring Tools. Courses were also resequenced.

Identifying Entry, Midpoint, Exit, and Continuing Points

You need to be able to identify the Entry, Midpoint, Exit, and Continuing benchmarks in your program. How do you assess at each point?

Criteria for the Entry point could include:

- undergraduate or Master's GPA

- score on the Miller's, GRE, or other required text

- interview

- performance test

- comprehensive exam

- written essay

- recommendations

How did you identify the Midpoint? The Midpoint does not have to be the exact middle of the program, credit-wise. The Midpoint indicator can be that course that reflects where a candidate should be, midway through the program. Criteria could include:

■ assessments in a course designated to be the Midpoint experience

■ portfolio at the midpoint

■ maintaining the required GPA

Criteria for the Exit point could include:

■ successfully completing the thesis or other capstone experience

■ successfully completing all courses

■ maintaining the required GPA

How did you identify Continuing benchmarks? Criteria could include:

■ surveys to alumni

■ surveys to employers

■ an active Alumni Association

■ regularly scheduled meetings of alumni, to provide feedback

Summary

Chapter 4 provided the administrative information to start organizing your accreditation process. The next step in the process is to ensure that everyone understands the ISTE TF and TL standards. This is the role of Chapters 5 and 6.

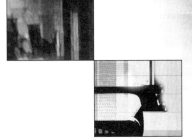

Unit Three

The Accreditation Process

chapter five

The Technology Facilitation Standards

The focus of Chapter 5 is to clarify your understanding of the TF standards and to illustrate how you can apply the standards to your program. This chapter connects the broader work of the previous section to a hands-on approach for developing a program that will be accredited.

One thing that you must remember for all eight standards is that it is not enough for your candidates to just demonstrate the use of technology. They have to meet each standard as stated.

At the end of each standard, an example called "Analyzing the Standard" will be presented, in which we select one indicator and help you understand what the key words are, who the audience is, and what activity should be assessed.

At the end of this chapter we will discuss common themes among the standards.

Standards and Indicators, with Analysis

The eight Technology Facilitation standards, indicated by Roman numerals, are:

I.   Technology Operations and Concepts

II.   Planning and Designing Learning Environments and Experiences

III. Teaching, Learning, and the Curriculum

IV.   Assessment and Evaluation

V.   Productivity and Professional Practice

VI.   Social, Ethical, Legal, and Human Issues

VII. Procedures, Policies, Planning, and Budgeting for Technology Environments

VIII. Leadership and Vision

Under each standard are indicators, represented by capital letters and Arabic numerals. For example, the first indicator of TF-I is TF-I.A.1:

> Assist teachers in the ongoing development of knowledge, skills, and understanding of technology systems, resources, and services that are aligned with district and state technology plans.

There are 78 indicators. On occasion ISTE refers to an indicator as a standard, which in essence it really is, because an indicator is really a specific part of the standard.

ISTE asks for you to collect eight assessments. A common misconception is that one assessment matches up with one standard. When you look at the standards and the indicators, you will see that many have common threads, or themes, that weave through several indicators from several standards and, therefore, can apply to the same assessment.

Technology Facilitation Standard I. (TF-I)

Technology Operations and Concepts. Educational technology facilitators demonstrate an in-depth understanding of technology operations and concepts.

Educational technology facilitators:

TF-I.A. Demonstrate knowledge, skills, and understanding of concepts related to technology (as described in the ISTE National Educational Technology Standards for Teachers).

Candidates:

1.   Assist teachers in the ongoing development of knowledge, skills, and understanding of technology systems, resources, and services that are aligned with district and state technology plans.

2. Provide assistance to teachers in identifying technology systems, resources, and services to meet specific learning needs.

TF-I.B. Demonstrate continual growth in technology knowledge and skills to stay abreast of current and emerging technologies.

Candidates:

1. Model appropriate strategies essential to continued growth and development of the understanding of technology operations and concepts.

Analyzing the Standard

TF-I.A.2. Provide assistance to teachers in identifying technology systems, resources, and services to meet specific learning needs.

In this case the focus of your candidates is on practicing teachers.

It is not enough for your candidates to use technology. You must demonstrate how candidates assist teachers with their use of technology to support student learning. For example, candidates assist teachers in recognizing and addressing use of assistive technology to provide accessibility to learning resources and familiarize teachers with assistive resources. Provide data and analysis. Is assistance provided through e-mail correspondence as well as face-to-face? How is the assistance delivered? Was a technology survey of practicing teachers used to determine the hardware and software preferred and the uses made of each? This is the assessment data indicating that candidates have demonstrated their capabilities.

Technology Facilitation Standard II. (TF-II)

Planning and Designing Learning Environments and Experiences. Educational technology facilitators plan, design, and model effective learning environments and multiple experiences supported by technology.

Educational technology facilitators:

TF-II.A. Design developmentally appropriate learning opportunities that apply technology-enhanced instructional strategies to support the diverse needs of learners.

Candidates:

1. Provide resources and feedback to teachers as they create developmentally appropriate curriculum units that use technology.

2. Consult with teachers as they design methods and strategies for teaching computer/technology concepts and skills within the context of classroom learning.

3. Assist teachers as they use technology resources and strategies to support the diverse needs of learners including adaptive and assistive technologies.

TF-II.B. Apply current research on teaching and learning with technology when planning learning environments and experiences.

Candidates:

1. Assist teachers as they apply current research on teaching and learning with technology when planning learning environments and experiences.

TF-II.C. Identify and locate technology resources and evaluate them for accuracy and suitability.

Candidates:

1. Assist teachers as they identify and locate technology resources and evaluate them for accuracy and suitability based on district and state standards.

2. Model technology integration using resources that reflect content standards.

TF-II.D. Plan for the management of technology resources within the context of learning activities.

Candidates:

1. Provide teachers with options for the management of technology resources within the context of learning activities.

TF-II.E. Plan strategies to manage student learning in a technology-enhanced environment.

Candidates:

1. Provide teachers with a variety of strategies to use to manage student learning in a technology-enhanced environment and support them as they implement the strategies.

TF-II.F. Identify and apply instructional design principles associated with the development of technology resources.

Candidates:

1. Assist teachers as they identify and apply instructional design principles associated with the development of technology resources.

Analyzing the Standard

TF-II.E.1. Provide teachers with a variety of strategies to use to manage candidate learning in a technology-enhanced environment and support them as they implement the strategies.

In this case the focus of your candidates is on practicing teachers.

Management concepts include arranging the technology for maximum use; dealing with access when there are fewer computers than students; grouping students for effective learning; signaling when help is needed; accessing limited printer resources; storing issues; and determining when technical assistance is necessary.

Teachers as Technology Leaders

It is not enough for your candidates to write a plan. You must demonstrate how candidates assist teachers. Provide data and analysis. Is assistance provided through professional development workshops? Web-enhanced learning? E-mail correspondence? How were needs determined? Was a survey of practicing teachers conducted? Where did the candidates obtain the knowledge to meet this standard? This is the assessment data indicating that candidates have demonstrated their capabilities.

Technology Facilitation Standard III. (TF-III)

Teaching, Learning, and the Curriculum. Educational technology facilitators apply and implement curriculum plans that include methods and strategies for utilizing technology to maximize student learning.

Educational technology facilitators:

TF-III.A. Facilitate technology-enhanced experiences that address content standards and student technology standards.

Candidates:

1. Use methods and strategies for teaching concepts and skills that support integration of technology productivity tools (refer to NETS for Students).

2. Use and apply major research findings and trends related to the use of technology in education to support integration throughout the curriculum.

3. Use methods and strategies for teaching concepts and skills that support integration of research tools (refer to NETS for Students).

4. Use methods and strategies for teaching concepts and skills that support integration of problem solving/decision-making tools (refer to NETS for Students).

5. Use methods and strategies for teaching concepts and skills that support use of media-based tools such as television, audio, print media, and graphics.

6. Use and describe methods and strategies for teaching concepts and skills that support use of distance learning systems appropriate in a school environment.

7. Use methods for teaching concepts and skills that support use of Web-based and non Web-based authoring tools in a school environment.

TF-III.B. Use technology to support learner-centered strategies that address the diverse needs of students.

Candidates:

1. Use methods and strategies for integrating technology resources that support the needs of diverse learners including adaptive and assistive technology.

TF-III.C. Apply technology to demonstrate students' higher-order skills and creativity.

Candidates:

1. Use methods and facilitate strategies for teaching problem-solving principles and skills using technology resources.

TF-III.D. Manage student learning activities in a technology-enhanced environment.

Candidates:

1. Use methods and classroom management strategies for teaching technology concepts and skills in individual, small group, classroom, and/or lab settings.

TF-III.E. Use current research and district/regional/state/national content and technology standards to build lessons and units of instruction.

Candidates:

1. Describe and identify curricular methods and strategies that are aligned with district/regional/state/national content and technology standards.

2. Use major research findings and trends related to the use of technology in education to support integration throughout the curriculum.

Analyzing the Standard

TF-III.A.4. Use methods and strategies for teaching concepts and skills that support integration of problem-solving/decision-making tools (refer to NETS for Students).

In this case the focus of your candidates is on students.

It is not enough for your candidates to teach or model the use of technology. You must demonstrate the requirements where candidates use problem-solving/decision-making tools to facilitate higher-order thinking among students. Are these tools integrated into project-based, problem-based, or inquiry-based activities? Problem-solving and decision-making tools could include spreadsheets, simulations, models, numeric modeling, concept-mapping, geometric manipulation, and demonstration software that should be addressed in this assessment.

How were the methods and strategies employed? How were mentoring, reinforcement, and enrichment provided? Provide data and analysis. This is the assessment data indicating that candidates have demonstrated their capabilities.

Technology Facilitation Standard IV. (TF-IV)

Assessment and Evaluation. Educational technology facilitators apply technology to facilitate a variety of effective assessment and evaluation strategies.

Educational technology facilitators:

TF-IV.A. Apply technology in assessing student learning of subject matter using a variety of assessment techniques.

Candidates:

1. Model the use of technology tools to assess student learning of subject matter using a variety of assessment techniques.

2. Assist teachers in using technology to improve learning and instruction through the evaluation and assessment of artifacts and data. [Note: Today, samples of candidates' work are called assessments. In the past, they were called artifacts.]

TF-IV.B. Use technology resources to collect and analyze data, interpret results, and communicate findings to improve instructional practice and maximize student learning.

Candidates:

1. Guide teachers as they use technology resources to collect and analyze data, interpret results, and communicate findings to improve instructional practice and maximize student learning.

TF-IV.C. Apply multiple methods of evaluation to determine students' appropriate use of technology resources for learning, communication, and productivity.

Candidates:

1. Assist teachers in using recommended evaluation strategies for improving students' use of technology resources for learning, communication, and productivity.

2. Examine and apply the results of a research project that includes evaluating the use of a specific technology in a P–12 environment.

Analyzing the Standard

TF-IV.C.1. Assist teachers in using recommended evaluation strategies for improving students' use of technology resources for learning, communication, and productivity.

In this case the focus of your candidates is on practicing teachers.

It is not enough for your candidates to write a rubric incorporating technology. You must demonstrate how candidates apply technology to facilitate a variety of effective assessment and evaluation strategies to assist teachers. For example, how is authentic assessment used in project-based, problem-based, and inquiry-based activities?

You need to demonstrate how the data collected, the research findings, and the analysis are integrated. Were there conferences with teachers to disseminate assessment and evaluation strategies? Assessment conferences could occur at institution/regional/ state teachers meetings. Were there online opportunities for conferences? How is the assistance delivered, via technology resources, to improve students' learning, communication, and productivity—and how can it be documented? This is the assessment data indicating that candidates have demonstrated their capabilities.

Technology Facilitation Standard V. (TF-V)

Productivity and Professional Practice. Educational technology facilitators apply technology to enhance and improve personal productivity and professional practice.

Educational technology facilitators:

TF-V.A. Use technology resources to engage in ongoing professional development and lifelong learning.

Candidates:

1. Identify resources and participate in professional development activities and professional technology organizations to support ongoing professional growth related to technology.

2. Disseminate information on district-wide policies for the professional growth opportunities for staff, faculty, and administrators.

TF-V.B. Continually evaluate and reflect on professional practice to make informed decisions regarding the use of technology in support of student learning.

Candidates:

1. Continually evaluate and reflect on professional practice to make informed decisions regarding the use of technology in support of student learning.

TF-V.C. Apply technology to increase productivity.

Candidates:

1. Model advanced features of word processing, desktop publishing, graphics programs, and utilities to develop professional products.

2. Assist others in locating, selecting, capturing, and integrating video and digital images in varying formats for use in presentations, publications and/or other products.

3. Demonstrate the use of specific-purpose electronic devices (such as graphing calculators, language translators, scientific probeware, or electronic thesaurus) in content areas.

4. Use a variety of distance learning systems and use at least one to support personal/professional development.

5. Use instructional design principles to develop hypermedia and multimedia products to support personal and professional development.

6. Select appropriate tools for communicating concepts, conducting research, and solving problems for an intended audience and purpose.

7. Use examples of emerging programming, authoring or problem-solving environments that support personal/professional development.

8. Set and manipulate preferences, defaults, and other selectable features of operating systems and productivity tool programs commonly found in P–12 schools.

TF-V.D. Use technology to communicate and collaborate with peers, parents, and the larger community in order to nurture student learning.

Candidates:

1. Model the use of telecommunications tools and resources for information sharing, remote information access, and multimedia/hypermedia publishing in order to nurture student learning.

2. Communicate with colleagues and discuss current research to support instruction, using applications including electronic mail, online conferencing, and Web browsers.

3. Participate in online collaborative curricular projects and team activities to build bodies of knowledge around specific topics.

4. Design, develop, and maintain Web pages and sites that support communication between the school and community.

Analyzing the Standard

TF-V.D.1. Model the use of telecommunications tools and resources for information sharing, remote information access, and multimedia/hypermedia publishing in order to nurture student learning.

In this case the focus of your candidates is on the members of the school community—peers, parents, and the larger community.

It is not enough for your candidates to use technology for their personal productivity, such as using a word processing program to type their lesson plans. You must demonstrate how candidates model its use for others to nurture student learning. For example, it is not enough to show that candidates are using telecommunications to communicate with peers, parents, and the community. Present how candidates are using telecommunications, remote access devices, hand-helds, publishing tools, and other tools to communicate information that has the potential to affect student learning. The student learning component must be documented by providing data and analysis. This is the assessment data indicating that candidates have demonstrated their capabilities.

Technology Facilitation Standard VI. (TF-VI)

Social, Ethical, Legal, and Human Issues. Educational technology facilitators understand the social, ethical, legal, and human issues surrounding the use of technology in P–12 schools and assist teachers in applying that understanding in their practice.

Educational technology facilitators:

TF-VI.A. Model and teach legal and ethical practice related to technology use.

Candidates:

1. Develop strategies and provide professional development at the school/classroom level for teaching social, ethical, and legal issues and responsible use of technology.

2. Assist others in summarizing copyright laws related to use of images, music, video, and other digital resources in varying formats.

TF-VI.B. Apply technology resources to enable and empower learners with diverse backgrounds, characteristics, and abilities.

Candidates:

1. Assist teachers in selecting and applying appropriate technology resources to enable and empower learners with diverse backgrounds, characteristics, and abilities.

2. Identify, classify, and recommend adaptive/assistive hardware and software for students and teachers with special needs and assist in procurement and implementation.

TF-VI.C. Identify and use technology resources that affirm diversity.

Candidates:

1. Assist teachers in selecting and applying appropriate technology resources to affirm diversity and address cultural and language differences.

TF-VI.D. Promote safe and healthy use of technology resources.

Candidates:

1. Assist teachers in selecting and applying appropriate technology resources to promote safe and healthy use of technology.

TF-VI.E. Facilitate equitable access to technology resources for all students.

Candidates:

1. Recommend policies and implement school/classroom strategies for achieving equitable access to technology resources for all students and teachers.

Analyzing the Standard

TF-VI.A.2. Assist others in summarizing copyright laws related to use of images, music, video, and other digital resources in varying formats.

In this case the focus of your candidates is on practicing teachers.

It is not enough for your candidates to demonstrate knowledge of copyright laws. You must demonstrate how candidates assist teachers in recognizing and addressing use of copyright laws and images, music, video, and other digital resources. Provide data and analysis. Is assistance provided through professional development workshops? Web-enhanced learning? E-mail correspondence? Was a survey used to determine practicing teachers' background knowledge and needs? Where did the candidates obtain the knowledge to meet this standard? Were materials prepared? Demonstrate where the candidates are assisting others. This is the assessment data indicating that candidates have demonstrated their capabilities.

Technology Facilitation Standard VII. (TF-VII)

Procedures, Policies, Planning, and Budgeting for Technology Environments. Educational technology facilitators promote the development and implementation of technology infrastructure, procedures, policies, plans, and budgets for P–12 schools.

Educational technology facilitators:

TF-VII.A. Use the school technology facilities and resources to implement classroom instruction.

Candidates:

1. Use plans to configure software/computer/technology systems and related peripherals in laboratory, classroom cluster, and other appropriate instructional arrangements.

2. Use local mass storage devices and media to store and retrieve information and resources.

3. Discuss issues related to selecting, installing, and maintaining wide area networks (WAN) for school districts.

4. Model integration of software used in classroom and administrative settings including productivity tools, information access/telecommunication tools, multimedia/hypermedia tools, school management tools, evaluation/portfolio tools, and computer-based instruction.

5. Utilize methods of installation, maintenance, inventory, and management of software libraries.

6. Use and apply strategies for troubleshooting and maintaining various hardware/software configurations found in school settings.

7. Use network software packages to operate a computer network system.

8. Work with technology support personnel to maximize the use of technology resources by administrators, teachers, and students to improve student learning.

TF-VII.B. Follow procedures and guidelines used in planning and purchasing technology resources.

Candidates:

1. Identify instructional software to support and enhance the school curriculum and develop recommendations for purchase.

2. Discuss and apply guidelines for budget planning and management procedures related to educational computing and technology facilities and resources.

3. Discuss and apply procedures related to troubleshooting and preventive maintenance of technology infrastructure.

4. Apply current information involving facilities planning issues and computer-related technologies.

5. Suggest policies and procedures concerning staging, scheduling, and security for managing computers/technology in a variety of school/laboratory/classroom settings.

6. Use distance and online learning facilities.

7. Describe and identify recommended specifications for purchasing technology systems in school settings.

TF-VII.C. Participate in professional development opportunities related to management of school facilities, technology resources, and purchases.

Candidates:

1. Support technology professional development at the building/school level utilizing adult learning theory.

Analyzing the Standard

TF-VII.B.5. Suggest policies and procedures concerning staging, scheduling, and security for managing computers/technology in a variety of school/laboratory/classroom settings.

In this case the focus of your candidates is on administrators and teachers.

It is not enough for your candidates to draw a floor plan for a computer room. You have to demonstrate how the candidates suggest policies and procedures in a variety of settings. The variety should include applications for K–12 classes as well as varied settings—laboratories, classrooms, and an overall school infrastructure. Provide data and analysis. The assessment should address not only classroom designs but also scheduling and security issues. A field experience shadowing activity or visits to other sites would enhance the technical, procedural, and administrative aspects for the candidates. This is the assessment data indicating that candidates have demonstrated their capabilities.

Technology Facilitation Standard VIII. (TF-VIII)

Leadership and Vision. Educational technology facilitators will contribute to the shared vision for campus integration of technology and foster an environment and culture conducive to the realization of the vision.

Educational technology facilitators:

TF-VIII.A. Use the school technology facilities and resources to implement classroom instruction.

Candidates:

1. Discuss and evaluate current research in educational technology.

TF-VIII.B. Apply strategies for and knowledge of issues related to managing the change process in schools.

Candidates:

1. Discuss the history of technology use in schools.

TF-VIII.C. Apply effective group process skills.

Candidates:

1. Discuss the rationale for forming school partnerships to support technology integration and examine an existing partnership within a school setting.

TF-VIII.D. Lead in the development and evaluation of district technology planning and implementation.

Candidates:

1. Participate in cooperative group processes and identify the processes that were effective.

2. Conduct an evaluation of a school technology environment.

3. Identify and discuss national, state, and local standards for integrating technology in the school environment.

4. Describe curriculum activities or performances that meet national, state, and local technology standards.

5. Discuss issues related to developing a school technology plan.

6. Discuss the elements of and strategies for developing a technology strategic plan.

7. Examine issues related to hardware and software acquisition and management.

TF-VIII.E. Engage in supervised field-based experiences with accomplished technology facilitators and/or directors.

Candidates:

1. Examine components needed for effective field-based experiences in instructional program development, professional development, facility and resource management, WAN/LAN/wireless systems, or managing change related to technology use in school-based settings.

Analyzing the Standard

TF-VIII. Educational technology facilitators will contribute to the shared vision for campus integration of technology and foster an environment and culture conducive to the realization of the vision.

In this case the focus of your candidates is on practicing teachers.

It is not enough for your candidates to write a vision statement or a long-range plan. You must demonstrate how candidates assist teachers. For example, candidates assist teachers in recognizing and addressing the use of assistive technology to provide accessibility to learning resources and familiarize teachers with assistive resources. Provide data and analysis. Is assistance provided through e-mail correspondence as well as face-to-face? How is the assistance delivered? Was an assistive technology survey of practicing teachers used to determine the hardware and software preferred and the uses made of each? This is the assessment data indicating that candidates have demonstrated their capabilities.

Common Themes

As you read the standards and indicators, one of the major aspects that you should notice is that there are common threads running through the indicators. They are not 78 segmented sentences. There are unifying features that, viewed together, create a complete and complex picture of a Technology Facilitator. We have selected four themes as examples: Modeling, Research, Diverse Needs of Learners, and Assistive Technology.

With these themes you can tie in your activities and assessments, as we will explore in the following chapter.

Theme: MODELING

Technology Operations and Concepts	**TF-I.B.1:** Model appropriate strategies essential to continued growth and development of the understanding of technology operations and concepts.
Planning and Designing Learning Environments and Experiences	**TF-II.C.2:** Model technology integration using resources that reflect content standards.
Assessment and Evaluation	**TF-IV.A.1:** Model the use of technology tools to assess student learning of subject matter using a variety of assessment techniques.
Productivity and Professional Practice	**TF-V.C.1:** Model advanced features of word processing, desktop publishing, graphics programs, and utilities to develop professional products. **TF-V.D.1:** Model the use of telecommunications tools and resources for information sharing, remote information access, and multimedia/hypermedia publishing in order to nurture student learning.
Social, Ethical, Legal, and Human Issues	**TF-VI.A:** Model and teach legal and ethical practice related to technology use.
Procedures, Policies, Planning, and Budgeting for Technology Environments	**TF-VII.A.4:** Model integration of software used in classroom and administrative settings including productivity tools, information access/telecommunication tools, multimedia/hypermedia tools, school management tools, evaluation/portfolio tools, and computer-based instruction.

Theme: RESEARCH

Planning and Designing Learning Environments and Experiences	**TF-II.B.1:** Assist teachers as they apply current research on teaching and learning with technology when planning learning environments and experiences.
Teaching, Learning, and the Curriculum	**TF-III.A.2:** Use and apply major research findings and trends related to the use of technology in education to support integration throughout the curriculum. **TF-III.A.3:** Use methods and strategies for teaching concepts and skills that support integration of research tools (refer to NETS for Students). **TF-III.E.2:** Use major research findings and trends related to the use of technology in education to support integration throughout the curriculum.

Theme: RESEARCH *(Continued)*

Assessment and Evaluation	**TF-IV.C.2:** Examine and apply the results of a research project that includes evaluating the use of a specific technology in a P–12 environment.
Productivity and Professional Practice	**TF-V.C.6:** Select appropriate tools for communicating concepts, conducting research, and solving problems for an intended audience and purpose. **TF-V.D.2:** Communicate with colleagues and discuss current research to support instruction, using applications including electronic mail, online conferencing, and Web browsers.
Leadership and Vision	**TF-VIII.A.1:** Discuss and evaluate current research in educational technology.

Theme: DIVERSE NEEDS OF LEARNERS

Planning and Designing Learning Environments and Experiences	**TF-II.A:** Design developmentally appropriate learning opportunities that apply technology-enhanced instructional strategies to support the diverse needs of learners. **TF-II.A.3:** Assist teachers as they use technology resources and strategies to support the diverse needs of learners including adaptive and assistive technologies.
Teaching, Learning, and the Curriculum	**TF-III.B:** Use technology to support learner-centered strategies that address the diverse needs of students. **TF-III.B.1:** Use methods and strategies for integrating technology resources that support the needs of diverse learners including adaptive and assistive technology.
Social, Ethical, Legal, and Human Issues	**TF-VI.B:** Apply technology resources to enable and empower learners with diverse backgrounds, characteristics, and abilities. **TF-VI.B.1:** Assist teachers in selecting and applying appropriate technology resources to enable and empower learners with diverse backgrounds, characteristics, and abilities.

Theme: ASSISTIVE TECHNOLOGY

Planning and Designing Learning Environments and Experiences	**TF-II.A.3:** Assist teachers as they use technology resources and strategies to support the diverse needs of learners including adaptive and assistive technologies.
Teaching, Learning, and the Curriculum	**TF-III.B.1:** Use methods and strategies for integrating technology resources that support the needs of diverse learners including adaptive and assistive technology.
Social, Ethical, Legal, and Human Issues	**TF-VI.B.2:** Identify, classify, and recommend adaptive/ assistive hardware and software for students and teachers with special needs and assist in procurement and implementation.

Summary

The TF standards are designed for candidates who wish to design, develop, and manage instructional materials through the use of educational technologies. Their primary role is to be a technology integration specialist—one who helps teachers integrate technology at the classroom level and manages professional development for schools. The school is their domain.

The TF program standards are aligned with the six National Educational Technology Standards for Teachers, but extend the performance expectations of each standard to reflect preparation in order to support student learning and educator professional growth with technology.

chapter six

The Technology Leadership Standards

The focus of Chapter 6 is to clarify your understanding of the TL standards and to illustrate how you can apply the standards to your program. Like Chapter 5, this chapter connects the broader work of Unit II to a hands-on approach for developing a successful program.

ISTE is consistent—like the TF Standards, it is not enough for your candidates to just demonstrate the use of technology. They have to meet each standard as stated.

In "Analyzing the Standard" we select one indicator and help you understand what the key words are, who the audience is, and what activity should be assessed.

Common themes, at the end of this chapter, demonstrates threads that run through all of the TL standards.

Standards and Indicators, with Analysis

The eight Technology Leadership standards, indicated by Roman numerals, are:

I.   Technology Operations and Concepts

II. Planning and Designing Learning Environments and Experiences

III. Teaching, Learning, and the Curriculum

IV. Assessment and Evaluation

V.   Productivity and Professional Practice

VI. Social, Ethical, Legal, and Human Issues

VII. Procedures, Policies, Planning, and Budgeting for Technology Environments

VIII. Leadership and Vision

Under each standard are indicators, represented by capital letters and Arabic numerals. For example, the first indicator of TL-I is TL-I.A.1:

> Identify and evaluate components needed for the continual growth of knowledge, skills, and understanding of concepts related to technology.

There are 78 indicators. On occasion ISTE refers to an indicator as a standard, which in essence it really is, because an indicator is really a specific part of the standard.

ISTE asks for you to collect eight assessments. A common misconception is that one assessment matches up with one standard. When you look at the standards and the indicators, you will see that many have common threads, or themes, that weave through several indicators from several standards and, therefore, can apply to the same assessment.

Technology Leadership Standard I. (TL-I)

Technology Operations and Concepts. Educational technology leaders demonstrate an advanced understanding of technology operations and concepts.

Educational technology leaders:

TL-I.A. Demonstrate knowledge, skills, and understanding of concepts related to technology (as described in the ISTE National Educational Technology Standards for Teachers).

Candidates:

1.   Identify and evaluate components needed for the continual growth of knowledge, skills, and understanding of concepts related to technology.

2.   Offer a variety of professional development opportunities that facilitate the ongoing development of knowledge, skills, and understanding of concepts related to technology.

TL-I.B. Demonstrate continual growth in technology knowledge and skills to stay abreast of current and emerging technologies.

Candidates:

1.   Offer a variety of professional development opportunities that facilitate the continued growth and development of the understanding of technology operations and concepts.

Analyzing the Standard

TL-I.B.1. Offer a variety of professional development opportunities that facilitate the continued growth and development of the understanding of technology operations and concepts.

In this case the focus of your candidates is on practicing teachers.

It is not enough for your candidates to use technology. You must demonstrate how candidates assist teachers through professional development to know how to be lifelong learners. For example, candidates should not only assist teachers in learning to use the SmartBoard but also how to integrate it effectively into the curriculum. Provide data and analysis. Is the professional development provided through Web-enhanced as well as face-to-face learning? How is the assistance delivered? Was a survey of practicing teachers used to determine the training that was needed? Was a survey used to determine the effectiveness of the training? This is the assessment data indicating that candidates have demonstrated their capabilities.

Technology Leadership Standard II. (TL-II)

Planning and Designing Learning Environments and Experiences. Educational technology leaders plan, design, and model effective learning environments and multiple experiences supported by technology.

Educational technology leaders:

TL-II.A. Design developmentally appropriate learning opportunities that apply technology-enhanced instructional strategies to support the diverse needs of learners.

Candidates:

1.   Research and disseminate project-based instructional units modeling appropriate uses of technology to support learning.

2. Identify and evaluate methods and strategies for teaching computer/technology concepts and skills within the context of classroom learning and coordinate dissemination of best practices at the district/state/regional level.

3. Stay abreast of current technology resources and strategies to support the diverse needs of learners including adaptive and assistive technologies and disseminate information to teachers.

TL-II.B. Apply current research on teaching and learning with technology when planning learning environments and experiences.

Candidates:

1. Locate and evaluate current research on teaching and learning with technology when planning learning environments and experiences.

TL-II.C. Identify and locate technology resources and evaluate them for accuracy and suitability.

Candidates:

1. Identify technology resources and evaluate them for accuracy and suitability based on the content standards.

2. Provide ongoing appropriate professional development to disseminate the use of technology resources that reflect content standards.

TL-II.D. Plan for the management of technology resources within the context of learning activities.

Candidates:

1. Identify and evaluate options for the management of technology resources within the context of learning activities.

TL-II.E. Plan strategies to manage student learning in a technology-enhanced environment.

Candidates:

1. Continually evaluate a variety of strategies to manage student learning in a technology-enhanced environment and disseminate through professional development activities.

TL-II.F. Identify and apply instructional design principles associated with the development of technology resources.

Candidates:

1. Identify and evaluate instructional design principles associated with the development of technology resources.

Analyzing the Standard

TL-II.F.1. Identify and evaluate instructional design principles associated with the development of technology resources.

In this case the focus of your candidates is on practicing teachers.

It is not enough for your candidates to find resources. You must demonstrate how candidates develop, implement and evaluate a professional development model to assist teachers in the identification and application of instructional design principles associated with the development of technology resources. Provide data and analysis. How were needs determined? Was a survey of practicing teachers conducted? Where did the candidates obtain the knowledge to meet this standard? This is the assessment data indicating that candidates have demonstrated their capabilities.

Technology Leadership Standard III. (TL-III)

Teaching, Learning, and the Curriculum. Educational technology leaders model, design, and disseminate curriculum plans that include methods and strategies for applying technology to maximize student learning.

Educational technology leaders:

TL-III.A. Facilitate technology-enhanced experiences that address content standards and student technology standards.

Candidates:

1. Design methods and strategies for teaching concepts and skills that support integration of technology productivity tools (refer to NETS for Students).

2. Design methods for teaching concepts and skills that support integration of communication tools (refer to NETS for Students).

3. Design methods and strategies for teaching concepts and skills that support integration of research tools (refer to NETS for Students).

4. Design methods and model strategies for teaching concepts and skills that support integration of problem-solving/decision-making tools (refer to NETS for Students).

5. Design methods and model strategies for teaching concepts and skills that support use of media-based tools such as television, audio, print media, and graphics.

6. Evaluate methods and strategies for teaching concepts and skills that support use of distance learning systems appropriate in a school environment.

7. Design methods and model strategies for teaching concepts and skills that support use of Web-based and non Web-based authoring tools in a school environment.

TL-III.B. Use technology to support learner-centered strategies that address the diverse needs of students.

Candidates:

1. Design methods and strategies for integrating technology resources that support the needs of diverse learners, including adaptive and assistive technology.

TL-III.C. Apply technology to demonstrate students' higher-order skills and creativity.

Candidates:

1. Design methods and model strategies for teaching hypermedia development, scripting, and/or computer programming, in a problem-solving context in the school environment.

TL-III.D. Manage student learning activities in a technology-enhanced environment.

Candidates:

1. Design methods and model classroom management strategies for teaching technology concepts and skills used in P–12 environments.

TL-III.E. Use current research and district/state/national content and technology standards to build lessons and units of instruction.

Candidates:

1. Disseminate curricular methods and strategies that are aligned with district/regional/state/national content and technology standards.

2. Investigate major research findings and trends relative to the use of technology in education to support integration throughout the curriculum.

Analyzing the Standard

TL-III.E.1. Disseminate curricular methods and strategies that are aligned with district/region/state/national content and technology standards.

In this case the focus of your candidates is on practicing teachers.

It is not enough for your candidates to simply disseminate information related to the use of technology in education. You must demonstrate how candidates support integration throughout the curriculum. How were the methods and strategies employed? How were mentoring, reinforcement, and enrichment provided? Provide data and analysis. This is the assessment data indicating that candidates have demonstrated their capabilities.

Technology Leadership Standard IV. (TL-IV)

Assessment and Evaluation. Educational technology leaders communicate research on the use of technology to implement effective assessment and evaluation strategies.

Educational technology leaders:

TL-IV.A. Apply technology in assessing student learning of subject matter using a variety of assessment techniques.

Candidates:

1. Facilitate the development of a variety of techniques to use technology to assess student learning of subject matter.

2. Provide technology resources for assessment and evaluation of artifacts and data.

TL-IV.B. Use technology resources to collect and analyze data, interpret results, and communicate findings to improve instructional practice and maximize student learning.

Candidates:

1. Identify and procure technology resources to aid in analysis and interpretation of data.

TL-IV.C. Apply multiple methods of evaluation to determine students' appropriate use of technology resources for learning, communication, and productivity.

Candidates:

1. Design strategies and methods for evaluating the effectiveness of technology resources for learning, communication, and productivity.

2. Conduct a research project that includes evaluating the use of a specific technology in P–12 environments.

Analyzing the Standard

TL-IV.A.1. Facilitate the development of a variety of techniques to use technology to assess student learning of subject matter.

In this case the focus of your candidates is on practicing teachers.

It is not enough for your candidates to research methods to assess student learning of subject matter using a variety of assessment techniques. You must demonstrate how candidates develop, implement, and assess innovative techniques that incorporate technology to facilitate a variety of effective assessment and evaluation strategies assist teachers.

You need to demonstrate how the data was developed, implemented, and assessed, and how the findings are integrated. Were there professional development workshops with teachers to disseminate these strategies? Were there online or one-to-one opportunities for conferences? How is the assistance delivered to improve student assessment—and how can it be documented? This is the assessment data indicating that candidates have demonstrated their capabilities.

Technology Leadership Standard V. (TL-V)

Productivity and Professional Practice. Educational technology leaders design, develop, evaluate and model products created using technology resources to improve and enhance their productivity and professional practice.

Educational technology leaders:

TL-V.A. Use technology resources to engage in ongoing professional development and lifelong learning.

Candidates:

1. Design, prepare, and conduct professional development activities to present at the school/district level and at professional technology conferences to support ongoing professional growth related to technology.

2. Plan and implement policies that support district-wide professional growth opportunities for staff, faculty, and administrators.

TL-V.B. Continually evaluate and reflect on professional practice to make informed decisions regarding the use of technology in support of student learning.

Candidates:

1. Based on evaluations make recommendations for changes in professional practices regarding the use of technology in support of student learning.

TL-V.C. Apply technology to increase productivity.

Candidates:

1. Model the integration of data from multiple software applications using advanced features of applications such as word processing, database, spreadsheet, communication, and other tools into a product.

2. Create multimedia presentations integrated with multiple types of data using advanced features of a presentation tool and model them to district staff using computer projection systems.

3. Document and assess field-based experiences and observations using specific-purpose electronic devices.

4. Use distance learning delivery systems to conduct and provide professional development opportunities for students, teachers, administrators, and staff.

5. Apply instructional design principles to develop and analyze substantive interactive multimedia computer-based instructional products.

6. Design and practice strategies for testing functions and evaluating technology use effectiveness of instructional products that were developed using multiple technology tools.

7. Analyze examples of emerging programming, authoring or problem-solving environments that support personal and professional development, and make recommendations for integration at school/district level.

8. Analyze and modify the features and preferences of major operating systems and/or productivity tool programs when developing products to solve problems.

TL-V.D. Use technology to communicate and collaborate with peers, parents, and the larger community in order to nurture student learning.

Candidates:

1. Model and implement the use of telecommunications tools and resources to foster and support information sharing, remote information access, and communication between students, school staff, parents, and local community.

2. Organize, coordinate, and participate in an online learning community related to the use of technology to support learning.

3. Organize and coordinate online collaborative curricular projects with corresponding team activities/responsibilities to build bodies of knowledge around specific topics.

4. Design, modify, maintain, and facilitate the development of Web pages and sites that support communication and information access between the entire school district and local/state/national/international communities.

Analyzing the Standard

TL-V.C.8. Analyze and modify the features and preferences of major operating systems and/or productivity tool programs when developing products to solve problems.

In this case the focus of your candidates is on the members of the school community—peers, parents, and the larger community.

It is not enough for your candidates to know how to use operating systems and productivity tools. You must demonstrate how candidates model its use for others, to nurture student learning. For example, it is not enough to show that candidates are using telecommunications to communicate with peers, parents, and the community. Present how candidates are using these tools to analyze, evaluate, and modify the features and preferences of the systems or programs when developing products to solve problems encountered with their operation and/or to enhance their capability. Where did the candidates obtain the knowledge to meet this standard? Demonstrate where the candidates are assisting others. This is the assessment data indicating that candidates have demonstrated their capabilities.

Technology Leadership Standard VI. (TL-VI)

Social, Ethical, Legal, and Human Issues. Educational technology leaders understand the social, ethical, legal, and human issues surrounding the use of technology in P–12 schools and develop programs facilitating application of that understanding in practice throughout their district/region/state.

Educational technology leaders:

TL-VI.A. Model and teach legal and ethical practice related to technology use.

Candidates:

1. Establish and communicate clear rules, policies, and procedures to support legal and ethical use of technologies at the district/regional/state levels.

2. Implement a plan for documenting adherence to copyright laws.

TL-VI.B. Apply technology resources to enable and empower learners with diverse backgrounds, characteristics, and abilities.

Candidates:

1. Communicate research on best practices related to applying appropriate technology resources to enable and empower learners with diverse backgrounds, characteristics, and abilities.

2. Develop policies and provide professional development related to acquisition and use of appropriate adaptive/assistive hardware and software for students and teachers with special needs.

TL-VI.C. Identify and use technology resources that affirm diversity.

Candidates:

1. Communicate research on best practices related to applying appropriate technology resources to affirm diversity and address cultural and language differences.

TL-VI.D. Promote safe and healthy use of technology resources.

Candidates:

1. Communicate research and establish policies to promote safe and healthy use of technology.

TL-VI.E. Facilitate equitable access to technology resources for all students.

Candidates:

1. Use research findings in establishing policy and implementation strategies to promote equitable access to technology resources for students and teachers.

Analyzing the Standard

TL-VI.E.1. Use research findings in establishing policy and implementation strategies to promote equitable access to technology resources for students and teachers.

In this case the focus of your candidates is on practicing teachers and students.

You must demonstrate how the research findings, the policies, and the implementation are integrated. How do candidates advocate national and international policies that provide equitable access to technology resources for all students and teachers? Conferences could occur at institution/regional/state teachers meetings. How is the assessment of the equitable access conducted? This is the assessment data indicating that candidates have demonstrated their capabilities.

Technology Leadership Standard VII. (TL-VII)

Procedures, Policies, Planning, and Budgeting for Technology Environments. Educational technology leaders coordinate development and direct implementation of technology infrastructure procedures, policies, plans, and budgets for P–12 schools.

Educational technology leaders:

TL-VII.A. Use the school technology facilities and resources to implement classroom instruction.

Candidates:

1. Develop plans to configure software/computer/technology systems and related peripherals in laboratory, classroom cluster, and other appropriate instructional arrangements.

2. Install local mass storage devices and media to store and retrieve information and resources.

3. Prioritize issues related to selecting, installing, and maintaining wide area networks (WAN) for school districts, and facilitate integration of technology infrastructure with the WAN.

4. Manage software used in classroom and administrative settings, including productivity tools, information access/telecommunication tools, multimedia/ hypermedia tools, school management tools, evaluation/portfolio tools, and computer-based instruction.

5. Evaluate methods of installation, maintenance, inventory, and management of software libraries.

6. Develop and disseminate strategies for troubleshooting and maintaining various hardware/software configurations found in school settings.

7. Select network software packages for operating a computer network system and/or local area network (LAN).

8. Analyze needs for technology support personnel to manage school/district technology resources and maximize use by administrators, teachers, and students to improve student learning.

TL-VII.B. Follow procedures and guidelines used in planning and purchasing technology resources.

Candidates:

1. Investigate purchasing strategies and procedures for acquiring administrative and instructional software for educational settings.

2. Develop and utilize guidelines for budget planning and management procedures related to educational computing and technology facilities and resources.

3. Develop and disseminate a system for analyzing and implementing procedures related to troubleshooting and preventive maintenance on technology infrastructure.

4. Maintain and disseminate current information involving facilities planning issues and computer-related technologies.

5. Design and develop policies and procedures concerning staging, scheduling, and security for managing hardware, software, and related technologies in a variety of instructional and administrative school settings.

6. Research and recommend systems and processes for implementation of distance learning facilities and infrastructure.

7. Differentiate among specifications for purchasing technology systems in school settings.

TL-VII.C. Participate in professional development opportunities related to management of school facilities, technology resources, and purchases.

Candidates:

1. Implement technology professional development at the school/district level utilizing adult learning theory.

Analyzing the Standard

TL-VII.B.3. Develop and disseminate a system for analyzing and implementing procedures related to troubleshooting and preventive maintenance of technology infrastructure.

In this case the focus of your candidates is on administrators and teachers.

It is not enough for your candidates to develop a plan. You must demonstrate how candidates operate a system for analyzing and implementing procedures related to troubleshooting and preventive maintenance on technology infrastructure. The variety should include applications for K–12 classes as well as varied settings—laboratories, classrooms, and an overall school infrastructure. Provide data and analysis. The analysis should address not only school applications but also scheduling and security issues. A field experience shadowing activity or visits to other sites would enhance the technical, procedural, and administrative aspects for the candidates. This is the assessment data indicating that candidates have demonstrated their capabilities.

Technology Leadership Standard VIII. (TL-VIII)

Leadership and Vision. Educational technology leaders will facilitate development of a shared vision for comprehensive integration of technology and foster an environment and culture conducive to the realization of the vision.

Educational technology leaders:

TL-VIII.A. Identify and apply educational and technology-related research, the psychology of learning, and instructional design principles in guiding the use of computers and technology in education.

Candidates:

1. Communicate and apply principles and practices of educational research in educational technology.

TL-VIII.B. Apply strategies for and knowledge of issues related to managing the change process in schools.

Candidates:

1. Describe social/historical foundations of education and how they relate to use of technology in schools.

TL-VIII.C. Apply effective group process skills.

Candidates:

1. Discuss issues relating to building collaborations, alliances, and partnerships involving educational technology initiatives.

TL-VIII.D. Lead in the development and evaluation of district technology planning and implementation.

Candidates:

1. Design and lead in the implementation of effective group process related to technology leadership or planning.

2. Use evaluation findings to recommend modifications in technology implementations.

3. Use national, state, and local standards to develop curriculum plans for integrating technology in the school environment.

4. Develop curriculum activities or performances that meet national, state, and local technology standards.

5. Compare and evaluate district-level technology plans.

6. Use strategic planning principles to lead and assist in the acquisition, implementation, and maintenance of technology resources.

7. Plan, develop, and implement strategies and procedures for resource acquisition and management of technology-based systems, including hardware and software.

TL-VIII.E. Engage in supervised field-based experiences with accomplished technology facilitators and/or directors.

Candidates:

1. Participate in a significant field-based activity involving experiences in instructional program development, professional development, facility and resource management, WAN/LAN/wireless systems, or managing change related to technology use in school-based settings.

Analyzing the Standard

TL-VIII.D.6. Use strategic planning principles to lead and assist in the acquisition, implementation, and maintenance of technology resources.

In this case the focus of your candidates is on the members of the school community—peers, parents, and the larger community.

It is not enough for your candidates to write a strategic plan. You must demonstrate how candidates assist the educational community. For example, candidates assist teachers by acquiring assistive technology through a grant; design professional development workshops for the implementation of these devices; and follow a policy for maintaining and securing these resources. Provide data and analysis. Is assistance provided through e-mail correspondence as well as face-to-face? How is the assistance delivered? Was a survey of teachers used to determine needed resources? How was the effectiveness of the strategic plan measured? This is the assessment data indicating that candidates have demonstrated their capabilities.

Common Themes

As you read the standards and indicators, one of the major aspects that you should notice is that there are common threads running through the indicators. They are not 78 segmented sentences. There are unifying features that, viewed together, create a complete and complex picture of a Technology Leader. We have selected four themes as examples: Evaluation, Professional Development, Design, and Implementation.

With these themes you can tie in your activities and assessments, as we will explore in the following chapter.

Theme: EVALUATION

Technology Operations and Concepts	**TL-I.A.1.** Identify and evaluate components needed for the continual growth of knowledge, skills, and understanding of concepts related to technology.
Planning and Designing Learning Environments and Experiences	**TL-II.A.2.** Identify and evaluate methods and strategies for teaching computer/technology concepts and skills within the context of classroom learning and coordinate dissemination of best practices at the district/state/regional level.
	TL-II.B.1. Locate and evaluate current research on teaching and learning with technology when planning learning environments and experiences.
	TL-II.C.1. Identify technology resources and evaluate them for accuracy and suitability based on the content standards.
	TL-II.D.1. Identify and evaluate options for the management of technology resources within the context of learning activities.
	TL-II.E.1. Continually evaluate a variety of strategies to manage student learning in a technology-enhanced environment and disseminate through professional development activities.
	TL-II.F.1. Identify and evaluate instructional design principles associated with the development of technology resources.
Teaching, Learning, and the Curriculum	**TL-III.A.6.** Evaluate methods and strategies for teaching concepts and skills that support use of distance learning systems appropriate in a school environment.

Theme: EVALUATION *(Continued)*

Assessment and Evaluation	**TL-IV.A.1:** Model the use of technology tools to assess student learning of subject matter using a variety of assessment techniques.
	TL-IV.C.1. Design strategies and methods for evaluating the effectiveness of technology resources for learning, communication, and productivity.
	TL-IV.C.2. Conduct a research project that includes evaluating use of a specific technology in a P–12 environment.
Productivity and Professional Practice	**TL-V.B.1.** Based on evaluations, make recommendations for changes in professional practices regarding the use of technology in support of student learning.
	TL-V.C.6. Design and practice strategies for testing functions and evaluating technology use effectiveness of instructional products that were developed using multiple technology tools.
Procedures, Policies, Planning, and Budgeting for Technology Environments	**TL-VII.A.5.** Model integration of software used in classroom and administrative settings, including productivity tools, information access/telecommunication tools, multimedia/ hypermedia tools, school management tools, evaluation/ portfolio tools, and computer-based instruction
Leadership and Vision	**TL-VIII.D.2.** Use evaluation findings to recommend modifications in technology implementations.
	TL-VIII.D.5. Compare and evaluate district-level technology plans.

Theme: PROFESSIONAL DEVELOPMENT

Technology Operations and Concepts	**TL-I.A.2.** Offer a variety of professional development opportunities that facilitate ongoing development of knowledge, skills, and understanding of concepts related to technology.
	TL-I.B.1. Offer a variety of professional development opportunities that facilitate continued growth and development of the understanding of technology operations and concepts.

Teachers as Technology Leaders

Theme: PROFESSIONAL DEVELOPMENT *(Continued)*

Planning and Designing Learning Environments and Experiences	**TL-II.C.2.** Provide ongoing appropriate professional development to disseminate use of technology resources that reflect content standards. **TL-II.E.1.** Continually evaluate a variety of strategies to manage student learning in a technology-enhanced environment and disseminate through professional development activities.
Productivity and Professional Practice	**TL-V.A.1.** Design, prepare, and conduct professional development activities to present at the school/district level and at professional technology conferences to support ongoing professional growth related to technology. **TL-V.A.2.** Plan and implement policies that support district-wide professional growth opportunities for staff, faculty, and administrators. **TL-V.C.4.** Use distance learning delivery systems to conduct and provide professional development opportunities for students, teachers, administrators, and staff. **TL-V.C.7.** Analyze examples of emerging programming, authoring or problem-solving environments that support personal and professional development, and make recommendations for integration at the school/district level.
Social, Ethical, Legal, and Human Issues	**TL-VI.B.2.** Develop policies and provide professional development related to acquisition and use of appropriate adaptive/assistive hardware and software for students and teachers with special needs.
Procedures, Policies, Planning, and Budgeting for Technology Environments	**TL-VII.C.1.** Implement technology professional development at the school/district level utilizing adult learning theory.
Leadership and Vision	**TL-VIII.E.1.** Participate in a significant field-based activity involving experiences in instructional program development, professional development, facility and resource management, WAN/LAN/wireless systems, or managing change related to technology use in school-based settings.

Theme: DESIGN

Planning and Designing Learning Environments and Experiences	**TL-II.A.** Design developmentally appropriate learning opportunities that apply technology-enhanced instructional strategies to support the diverse needs of learners.
	TL-II.F. Identify and apply instructional design principles associated with the development of technology resources.
Teaching, Learning, and the Curriculum	**TL-III.A.1.** Design methods and strategies for teaching concepts and skills that support integration of technology productivity tools (refer to NETS for Students).
	TL-III.A.2. Design methods for teaching concepts and skills that support integration of communication tools (refer to NETS for Students).
	TL-III.A.3. Design methods and strategies for teaching concepts and skills that support integration of research tools (refer to NETS for Students).
	TL-III.A.4. Design methods and model strategies for teaching concepts and skills that support integration of problem-solving/decision-making tools (refer to NETS for Students).
	TL-III.A.5. Design methods and model strategies for teaching concepts and skills that support use of media-based tools such as television, audio, print media, and graphics.
	TL-III.A.7. Design methods and model strategies for teaching concepts and skills that support use of Web-based and non Web-based authoring tools in a school environment.
	TL-III.B.1. Design methods and strategies for integrating technology resources that support the needs of diverse learners including adaptive and assistive technology.
	TL-III.C.1. Design methods and model strategies for teaching hypermedia development, scripting, and/or computer programming, in a problem-solving context in the school environment.
	TL-III.D.1. Design methods and model classroom management strategies for teaching technology concepts and skills used in P–12 environments.
Assessment and Evaluation	**TL-IV.C.1.** Design strategies and methods for evaluating the effectiveness of technology resources for learning, communication, and productivity.

Teachers as Technology Leaders

Theme: DESIGN *(Continued)*

Productivity and Professional Practice	**TL-V.A.1.** Design, prepare, and conduct professional development activities to present at the school/district level and at professional technology conferences to support ongoing professional growth related to technology.
	TL-V.C.6. Design and practice strategies for testing functions and evaluating technology use effectiveness of instructional products that were developed using multiple technology tools.
	TL-V.D.4. Design, modify, maintain, and facilitate the development of Web pages and sites that support communication and information access between the entire school district and local/state/national/international communities.
Procedures, Policies, Planning, and Budgeting for Technology Environments	**TL-VII.B.5.** Design and develop policies and procedures concerning staging, scheduling, and security for managing hardware, software, and related technologies in a variety of instructional and administrative school settings.
Leadership and Vision	**TL-VIII.D.1.** Design and lead in the implementation of effective group process related to technology leadership or planning.

Theme: IMPLEMENTATION

Productivity and Professional Practice	**TL-V.A.2.** Plan and implement policies that support district-wide professional growth opportunities for staff, faculty, and administrators.
	TL-V.D.1. Model and implement use of telecommunications tools and resources to foster and support information sharing, remote information access, and communication between students, school staff, parents, and local community.
Social, Ethical, Legal, and Human Issues	**TL-VI.A.2.** Implement a plan for documenting adherence to copyright laws.
	TL-VI.E.1. Use research findings in establishing policy and implementation strategies to promote equitable access to technology resources for students and teachers.

Theme: IMPLEMENTATION (Continued)

Procedures, Policies, Planning, and Budgeting for Technology Environments	**TL-VII.A.** Use the school technology facilities and resources to implement classroom instruction. **TL-VII.B.3.** Develop and disseminate a system for analyzing and implementing procedures related to troubleshooting and preventive maintenance on technology infrastructure. **TL-VII.B.6.** Research and recommend systems and processes for implementation of distance learning facilities and infrastructure. **TL-VII.C.1.** Implement technology professional development at the school/district level utilizing adult learning theory.
Leadership and Vision	**TL-VIII.D.** Lead in the development and evaluation of district technology planning and implementation. **TL-VIII.D.1.** Design and lead in the implementation of effective group process related to technology leadership or planning. **TL-VIII.D.2.** Use evaluation findings to recommend modifications in technology implementations. **TL-VIII.D.6.** Use strategic planning principles to lead and assist in the acquisition, implementation, and maintenance of technology resources. **TL-VIII.D.7.** Plan, develop, and implement strategies and procedures for resource acquisition and management of technology-based systems, including hardware and software.

Summary

The TL standards are designed to communicate expectations for the performance of candidates who will serve as Educational Computing and Technology Directors, Coordinators, or Specialists at the district, regional, and/or state levels. This responsibility takes many forms within the varying environments across educational systems.

In Chapters 5 and 6 we looked at the 8 Standards and the 78 Indicators that comprise the TF and the TL standards. In the last section of both chapters, Common Themes, we saw that there are threads running through the indicators. In Chapter 7, we will explain how you develop your assessments. Seeing common themes will make it easier for you to assemble the assessments required by ISTE.

chapter seven

Developing the Assessments

The focus of this chapter is to show you how to develop your assessments. As you learned in Chapters 5 and 6, seeing common themes makes it easier for you to assemble the eight TF or TL assessments required by ISTE:

Assessment 1. Program entry-level benchmark, or licensure tests or professional examinations of content knowledge [Entry-Level Assessment]

Assessment 2. Assessment of content knowledge in the field of educational technology leadership [Leadership Assessment]

Assessment 3. Assessment that demonstrates candidates can collaborate effectively; plan, design, and model effective learning environments; and plan and implement professional experiences required of a technology leader [Designing Assessment]

Assessment 4. Assessment that demonstrates candidates' knowledge, skills, and dispositions are applied effectively in practice [Professional Practice Assessment]

Assessment 5. Assessment that demonstrates the candidate models, designs, and disseminates methods and strategies in technology that enhance student learning [Student Learning Assessment]

Assessment 6. Assessment that demonstrates the candidate understands and can develop programs that address the social, legal and ethical issues related to technology within the district/region/state [Ethical Assessment]

Assessment 7. Assessment that addresses how the candidate uses technology to plan and implement effective assessment and evaluation strategies [Evaluation Assessment]

Assessment 8. Assessment that addresses facilitation of a shared vision for integration of technology and how to foster an environment and culture conducive to the realization of the vision [Vision Assessment]

Introduction to Assessment

To understand the current framework of an eight-assessment system, a little history is helpful. Previously, the requirements and reports from the different Specialized Professional Associations (SPAs) were tailored to the individual scope and standards of each organization. The process of making the SPA reports consistent was an initiative of NCATE in 2003 because the program review process was seen "in great need of simplification and redesign" (Farstrup, 2004). The NCATE Executive Board organized a taskforce to review the process. Among other recommendations, it was decided that the reports from the various SPAs would be consistent and would directly correlate to NCATE Standard I in content and terminology (Farstrup, 2004). NCATE Standard I reads:

> Candidates preparing to work in schools as teachers or other professional school personnel know and demonstrate the content, pedagogical, and professional knowledge, skills, and dispositions necessary to help all students learn. Assessments indicate that candidates meet professional, state, and institutional standards.

The current report requirements can be considered to be a hybrid of the TF and the TL standards, the focus and language of NCATE Standard I, and common elements of the major SPAs affiliated with NCATE.

It is important to understand the distinctions and relationships among assessments. There are three types of interrelated assessments in the NCATE process—candidate assessments, program assessments, and Unit assessments.

Candidate assessments are those given to audit or provide feedback to the candidate. This can be a quiz, a test, a project with scored rubric, and/or a portfolio. It is the type of work crucial to the teaching of a course.

Program assessments are based on assessments from the candidates although the direct goal is to measure and evaluate your program, not to measure, audit, or provide feedback to the candidate. These can be individual candidate assessments or amalgams of candidate assessments. They are selected and culled because they speak for the work of the entire program, and they are based on experiences that every candidate shares. Program assessments are the focus of this book and of the TF and the TL accreditation processes.

The Unit assessment system is the larger assessment system that your institution has. Your program contributes data to this Unit assessment system. Several of the candidate and program assessments may be a part of the Unit assessment. There might also be assessments superimposed on your candidates or program to obtain data for your Unit assessment. A Unit-wide survey that your program distributes to your candidates would fall into this category. The data for the ISTE TF and TL reports focus on program assessments, which are derived from candidate assessments.

The number of assessments that you are required to submit for your program assessment depends on the due date of your report. The due date of your report is dependent upon the date of the NCATE visit to your institution. The information below is from NCATE (February 6, 2006).

Assessment Data

For program report submissions between Fall 2004 and Spring 2007, if the program has at least one semester's data on at least five assessments, the SPA standards are met, and the assessments are adequate, the program can be nationally recognized. If one semester's data are available for less than five assessments, the program could be nationally recognized with conditions. The following chart outlines the amount of data required for program reports submitted through Fall 2009. After Fall 2009, the minimum expectation is three years of data.

TABLE 3 ■ Required data.

AMOUNT OF DATA REQUIRED FOR PROGRAM REVIEWS AND SITE VISITS			
Program Reports Submitted	Amount of Data Required	Site Visit Date	Amount of Data Required
Through February 1, 2007	1 semester	Through Spring 2008	1 year
September 15, 2007	1 year	Fall 2008	2 years
February 1, 2008	1 year	Spring 2009	2 years
September 15, 2008	2 years	Fall 2009	3 years
February 1, 2009	2 years	Spring 2010	3 years
September 15, 2009 and afterwards	3 years	Fall 2010 and afterwards	3 years

NCATE (2006)

Candidate Assessments

An excellent program is based on meaningful experiences for your candidates. The main source of evaluation data will be your candidate assessments; the eight program assessments will be a purposeful and intelligent selection of combined and individual candidate assessments. With the exception of entry requirements and field experiences, the majority of your candidates' assessments will come from work done in courses; therefore, it is crucial for you to develop engaging and relevant assignments with clear and helpful assessments based on the standards.

When developing candidate assessments it is imperative to not only look at the TF or the TL standards, but also at the TF (http://cnets.iste.org/ncate/n_fac-rubrics.html) and the TL (http://cnets.iste.org/ncate/n_lead-rubrics.html) rubrics. Many of the rubric items vary qualitatively and substantively among the Approaches, Meets, and Exceeds categories. **These rubrics are excellent guides for the development of programs, courses, projects, and assessments, but they can be an inconsistent "fit" to assess candidates directly, especially for anchored projects or authentic assessment.** For example, look at the Rubric for standard TF-I.A.1:

> Assist teachers in the ongoing development of knowledge, skills, and understanding of technology systems, resources, and services that are aligned with district and state technology plans.

TABLE 4 ■ Sample rubric.

	APPROACHES	MEETS	EXCEEDS
TF-I.A.1	Make appropriate choices about technology systems, resources, and services that are aligned with district and state standards.	Assist teachers in the ongoing development of knowledge, skills, and understanding of technology systems, resources, and services that are aligned with district and state technology plans.	Conduct needs assessment to determine baseline data on teachers' knowledge, skills, and understanding of concepts related to technology.

The TF standard is the "Meets" criterion. It would be a relatively straightforward task to develop a project and assessment based on this criterion. However, taken in its entirety, the above three criteria of Approaches, Meets and Exceeds would be vague guidance and a poor assessment tool for many projects or assignments—each category of Approaches, Meets, and Exceeds relates to substantively different activities. This becomes especially salient in activities that are based on professional practice and authentic activities which would address several interrelated standards.

To address these issues we recommend a process with four interrelated components for the creation of standards-based performance criteria for candidate assessment:

1. Commitment to peer review. Developing projects and assessments should be a collaborative process with one faculty member taking the lead in presenting a project, exam, or assessment. Other faculty members and stakeholders are reviewers, improving the clarity and rigor of the projects, the correlation to the targeted standards, and the appropriateness of the performance criteria.

2. Based on the place of the assessment in the program (beginning, middle, or end) and the context of the assessment (such as a field experience or an anchored project), you should choose the **Meets** or **Exceeds criterion** from the ISTE Rubric. An assessment early in the program might warrant targeting the Meets criterion, while an assessment later in the program could well target the Exceeds criterion. A project that has the candidates performing an anchored, purposeful project such as mentoring teachers or conducting a professional development workshop would likely address a specific level of Meets or Exceeds of a particular standard. Complex professional tasks that are situated in authentic activities naturally address particular standards on either the Meets or Exceeds criterion. For example, a project that requires a needs assessment would address the Exceeds criterion of TF-I.A.1.

3. Whether you begin with the standards or an existing assessment, creating meaningful projects and assessments involves revision. You will have to continually refine the assessment, including the instructions to the candidate and the scoring criteria; this might include adding or removing standards as well as revising the scoring criteria. Adult learning theory is premised on giving candidates meaningful and purposeful activities. This involves considering the local context and giving students some degree of choice. Developing activities that engage your candidates, writing clear instructions and assessments, and addressing specific standards are pieces that do not immediately "fit." It takes work and revision to develop meaningful, standards-based tasks.

4. Develop specific performance expectations that are clearly derived from and correlated to the standard. The example below is taken from a course assessment that requires candidates to conduct a needs assessment and design a subsequent professional development project. We chose the Exceeds criterion of the rubric from ISTE TF-I.A.1 (see table 4). This assessment gives candidates clear objectives to meet the standards that are derived from the standard itself and the requirements of the task. Subsequently, you can develop a relevant scale to assess candidates' performance on these criteria.

TABLE 5 ■ Performance expectation.

ISTE STANDARD— RUBRIC EXCEEDS	ASSESSMENT PERFORMANCE CRITERIA
TF-I.A.1. Conduct needs assessment to determine baseline data on teachers' knowledge, skills, and understanding of concepts related to technology.	An assessment is given to at least eight teachers of a particular subject/grade in a school or district. The assessment clearly ascertains the general technical experience and the specific knowledge of the teachers on the topic. Assessment also identifies level and experience with technology integration.

We suggest a four-tiered scale of "Unacceptable," "Emerging," "Satisfactory," and "Exemplary" in which we describe the performance this way:

Exemplary. Candidate demonstrates a thorough understanding of the knowledge, skills, and dispositions. Candidate has completed all of the performance criteria in a professional way (well written, well formatted, on time).

Satisfactory. Candidate demonstrates a clear understanding of the knowledge, skills, and dispositions. Candidate has completed most/all of the performance criteria with some deviation from professional standards.

Emerging. Candidate demonstrates an incomplete but burgeoning understanding of the knowledge, skills, and dispositions. Candidate has completed some of the performance criteria with some major deviations from professional standards.

Unacceptable. Candidate demonstrates an incomplete and/or misguided understanding of the knowledge, skills, and dispositions. Candidate has completed little/none of the performance criteria.

We then give a raw score of 0 (Unacceptable) to 3 (Exemplary) for each performance criterion and related standard. Unlike other assessment systems that avoid negative terms like unacceptable, we believe that part of developing an appropriate disposition is an understanding that there is work and conduct that cannot and should not be a part of professional performance. This threshold is expected to get higher as the candidate advances through the program. We also prefer the term "Exemplary" to "Exceeds" to indicate the highest level of performance. Exemplary means that the candidate has done an excellent job at performance criteria as delineated in the assessment and there was no extra credit or need for the candidate to guess how to go above and beyond.

There has been a trend to avoid the terms validity and reliability in candidate assessment because of the psychometric implications of those terms. However, you should strive to make your assessments fair. Fairness implies that the candidates have the support and resources to complete the assignment. For example, you would not expect candidates to participate in a workshop or to purchase expensive software without a reasonable amount of advance notice. Fairness also implies that the assessment score reflects the performance of the task. This can be addressed in the four-step process above. Be aware that a common pitfall is that many tasks do not involve proportionally weighing the individual scoring items. For example, if you assign a research paper and your criteria are formatting, written expression, and content, your final score would likely weigh content more than written expression and written expression more than formatting. Finally, your assessments need to be transparent. Candidates should be given clear instructions, the grading policy, and the rubric before they begin the assignment.

Program Assessments

Now that we have looked at the standards in detail, you should understand how they relate to the assessment of your program. In the next chapter we will cover how assessments integrate into your accreditation report.

ISTE accreditation requires a program assessment system comprised of eight assessments though, as stated previously, this number can vary depending on the time of submission. These assessments must be experiences or course assessments completed by every candidate in your program. If there are electives in your program, assessments completed in these courses are not included because they are not completed by every candidate.

Your assessment system and report have to address the indicators for all eight standards. For the TF Standards there are eight Standards with 33 Indicators and 78 discrete standards. For the TL Standards there are eight Standards with 33 Indicators and 78 discrete standards. We have labeled the components in **BOLD CAPS** in the example below:

> **Standard I.** Educational technology facilitators demonstrate an in-depth understanding of technology operations and concepts. (**STANDARD**)
>
> Educational technology facilitators:
>
> **TF-I.A.** Demonstrate knowledge, skills, and understanding of concepts related to technology (as described in the ISTE National Educational Technology Standards for Teachers). (**INDICATOR**)
>
> Candidates:
>
> 1. Assist teachers in the ongoing development of knowledge, skills, and understanding of technology systems, resources, and services that are aligned with district and state technology plans. (**DISCRETE STANDARD**)
>
> 2. Provide assistance to teachers in identifying technology systems, resources, and services to meet specific learning needs. (**DISCRETE STANDARD**)

For the accreditation report you are required to **address the indicator**, not the larger eight standards directly or the discrete standards. Your assessment system has to target the 33 TF or the 33 TL indicators, not the 78 TF and TL discrete standards. The discrete standards should be viewed as guidance for the development of your assessments and program.

When you address the indicator and there is only one discrete standard, the criteria for passing that indicator is clear. However, when there are multiple discrete standards for an indicator, you must use the discrete standards as guidance in the development of the assessment. Targeting all 78 of the discrete standards in your assessment system may be impractical or even counterproductive for an authentic assessment.

The excerpt below is from the Reviewers' Report (NCATE, 2006) used to assess your Report for Accreditation. It is how the reviewers will evaluate your submission.

TL-III. Teaching, Learning, and the Curriculum.

Educational technology leaders model, design, and disseminate curriculum plans that include methods and strategies for applying technology to maximize student learning. Educational technology leaders will:

A. Facilitate technology-enhanced experiences that address content standards and student technology standards.

	MET	NOT MET
1. Design methods and strategies for teaching concepts and skills that support integration of technology productivity tools (refer to NETS for Students).	☐	☐
2. Design methods for teaching concepts and skills that support integration of communication tools (refer to NETS for Students).	☐	☐
3. Design methods and strategies for teaching concepts and skills that support integration of research tools (refer to NETS for Students).	☐	☐
4. Design methods and model strategies for teaching concepts and skills that support integration of problem-solving/ decision-making tools (refer to NETS for Students).	☐	☐
5. Design methods and model strategies for teaching concepts and skills that support use of media-based tools such as television, audio, print media, and graphics.	☐	☐
6. Evaluate methods and strategies for teaching concepts and skills that support use of distance learning systems appropriate in a school environment.	☐	☐
7. Design methods and model strategies for teaching concepts and skills that support use of Web-based and non Web-based authoring tools in a school environment.	☐	☐

COMMENT:

B. Use technology to support learner-centered strategies that address the diverse needs of students.

	MET	NOT MET
1. Design methods and strategies for integrating technology resources that support the needs of diverse learners including adaptive and assistive technology.	☐	☐

COMMENT:

Notice how the indicator for TL Standard III.A has 7 discrete indicators and TL Standard III.B has only 1. Addressing TL-III.B is relatively straightforward because indicator TL-III.B is solely measured by discrete standard TL-III.B.1. This correlates to Section III of the Accreditation Report as well (which we will cover later).

We recommend a reflective and commonsensical approach to developing assessments for indicators with many discrete standards (example TL-III.A above). You need to look at the experience that you are assessing for the candidate. Does your description of the assessment convey a substantive experience that embodies the indicator and correlates with the *sense* and themes of the discrete standards?

The eight assessments in your assessment directly address Sections II, III, and IV of the TL or the TF accreditation reports and are discussed in detail in the next chapter. Assessment instruments can include papers, projects, surveys, interviews, portfolios, and exams. This is not to say that smaller, formative assessments such as quizzes or short papers have no place here. If they assess a crucial skill, they can be incorporated into a larger assessment such as an exam, unit evaluation, course assessment, or portfolio. Any or all of the eight assessments can be a combination of other assessments. In its guidance to SPAs and programs, NCATE (2006) clarifies the composition of these assessments as:

> A single key assessment could include several components, or 'sub-assessments.' For example, an assessment of candidate impact on student learning could include a pre-test, unit plan, implementation of unit plan, post-test and reflection. Each of these components may be evaluated and scored individually, with a final score computed from the sub-scores.

A portfolio is an excellent example of this. You could also have a comprehensive assessment, which could be a purposeful and coherent collection of smaller assessments with appropriate scoring criteria. For example, a comprehensive assessment could include a quiz, a response paper, and a project. The key to the assessment system is for the comprehensive assessment to yield a single score.

The suggestions here focus on exams, portfolios, projects, and research papers. Below is a list of assessments that could fit into your system.

- Interviews
- Observations
- Reaction Papers
- Quizzes
- Observations of Field Experiences
- Online Discussions
- Classroom Discussions
- Unit Assessment

Remember, each assessment must have clear and credible scoring criteria—typically, a rubric with criteria from the ISTE or the TF rubric.

Here are the eight TF and TL assessments designed by ISTE. For each assessment we provide a commentary followed by a discussion related to the TF and the TL standards.

Assessment 1: ENTRY-LEVEL ASSESSMENT

Program entry-level benchmark, or licensure tests or professional examinations of content knowledge

Commentary

This entry-level benchmark is designed to ensure that candidates come in with the prerequisites to work on the TF and the TL materials. There have been occasions in many programs when a candidate lacks the background knowledge to successfully begin. The key to this assessment is that the candidate can "hit the ground running" in the program. If there is a state licensure test for technology facilitator or leader, these results should be used. However, this is rarely the case. We would recommend using acceptance criteria for your program such as a portfolio or entrance exam. There could also be a skills test in an introductory course in which those who do not meet the criteria could be offered a remediation program to get the requisite skills.

For TF	ISTE correlates this assessment to TF-I and the general sense of this standard is that candidates must have the knowledge of the NETS•T. Both indicators and all of the discrete standards of TF-I relate to the NETS•T. An assessment that gauges entry-level competence to begin a TF program is appropriate.
For TL	ISTE suggests that this assessment focus on Standard TL-I. The two indicators of this standard embody the NETS•T and the TF standards. TL-I.A directly refers to the knowledge and skills as described in the NETS•T; and TL-I.B refers to continual growth in technology knowledge and the ability to stay abreast of current and emerging technologies. TL-I.B has only one discrete standard and this is to "Offer a variety of professional development opportunities that facilitate the continued growth and development of the understanding of technology operations and concepts" (TL-I.B.1). This discrete indicator embodies the sense of the TF standards.

Assessment 2: CONTENT KNOWLEDGE ASSESSMENT

Assessment of content knowledge in the field

Commentary

Of all of the assessments, this is one of the broadest. For both the TF and the TL standards, much of the knowledge is integrated with skills and dispositions, so this assessment can apply to almost any standard or indicator. Both reports suggest Standards I through VIII for this assessment. When developing your assessments, it would be a helpful idea to create or revise this one last. You can see what standards and indicators you have missed with the other assessments, which are much more targeted.

For TF	For the TF accreditation this assessment will assess the content knowledge for Technology Facilitation.
For TL	For the TL accreditation this assessment will assess the content knowledge for Technology Leadership.

Assessment 3: PLANNING ASSESSMENT

Pedagogical and professional knowledge, skills, and dispositions

Commentary

This assessment emphasizes planning, collaboration, and implementation of professional experiences.

For TF	The TF report focuses on collaboration with classroom teachers. The report suggests Standards II, V, VI, VII, and VIII. Assessments could include projects that involve planning school-based activities in collaboration with teachers; professional development projects, developing curriculum, or technology plans with various stakeholders. All work should be correlated to state and national standards such as the NETS•T, NETS•S, and your state's curriculum content standards. The actual assessments can be reports on these projects. To engage and assess candidate collaboration, the projects can include notes from focus groups with teachers, a survey collection, and the aggregation and analysis of such data.
For TL	The TL assessment focuses on work with teachers, administrators, and parent groups. Activities can include the creation of professional development workshops, district-wide technology plans, research-based analysis of a district's technology infrastructure, or a district-wide needs assessments. Work should be correlated to relevant standards including the NETS•S, NETS•T, and NETS•A.

Assessment 4: PROFESSIONAL PRACTICE ASSESSMENT

Assessment that demonstrates candidates' knowledge, skills, and dispositions are applied effectively in practice

Commentary

This assessment focuses on the application of knowledge, skills, and dispositions. The source of this data should be field experiences, either individual courses or experiences and projects embedded in courses that have a field experience component. For field assessments for TL or TF, a project that directly correlates to a majority of the discrete standards would be extremely useful. For example, you can list a series of discrete standards in designing the tasks for performance and reflection in a field experience.

For TF	ISTE suggests Standards II through VIII for this. Ideal assessments would be action research projects, evaluations of field experiences or mentoring projects, implementation of professional development experiences.
For TL	ISTE suggests Standard V for this. Standard TL-V is "Productivity and Professional Practice" and has three indicators relating to professional development, student learning, and productivity. The assessments can be results from professional development projects, and internship reports. You could target discrete standards when developing a project and candidate assessment for internship experiences or developing professional development workshops.

Assessment 5: STUDENT LEARNING ASSESSMENT

Assessment that demonstrates the candidate models, designs, and disseminates methods and strategies in technology that enhance student learning

Commentary

Ironically, this can be one of the most difficult assessments to measure, but it is one of the most important. This assessment is geared towards students—typically students in P–12 learning environments. This is at the heart of what we do as teacher educators. How are your current candidates reaching students through their work with teachers, administrators, and parents? The important element is data from and about students.

For TF	ISTE recommends Standards II, III, IV, V, VI, and VIII. The candidates need to demonstrate that they have the skills to implement curriculum plans that get teachers to use technology to enhance student learning. For a candidate this can be specific to a grade and subject or run the spectrum of student ages and subjects. The types of assessment can include portfolios, case studies, or longitudinal studies. The student and candidate work should be correlated to the NETS•S.
For TL	ISTE recommends TL Standard III for this. Because the TL programs focus on the district and school level it is somewhat removed from the day-to-day work of students. It is a mistake to have the student learning in the forefront of a TL's work and mission. Demonstrating the knowledge and skills to improve student learning has to be ingrained as a disposition for your candidates. Assessments could include evaluations of student learning with specific technologies, nature of school Internet use, case studies of student technology use, and student portfolios.

Assessment 6: ETHICAL ASSESSMENT

Assessment that demonstrates the candidate understands and can develop programs that address the social, legal and ethical issues related to technology within the district/region/state

Commentary

Assessing the social, legal and ethical components of a candidate's education is one of the more distinct topics in the eight-part assessment system. Many of the other assessments can overlap or can correlate to various combinations of standards and indicators. This assessment strongly correlates to Standard VI of both the TF and the TL standards.

For TF	TF Standard VI should be targeted in this assessment. Along with TF-VI.B, indicators TF-II.A and TF-III.B address assistive and adaptive technology, so these three indicators can be assessed together. A strong assessment would be for the candidates to develop a workshop series (2 to 3 workshops and related support) on social, legal, and ethical issues of educational technology. This should include information on assistive and adaptive technologies.
For TL	TL Standard VI should be targeted in this assessment. Experiences and assessments can have candidates developing acceptable use or safety and security policies, as well as addressing copyright and fair use issues.

Assessment 7: EVALUATION ASSESSMENT

Assessment that addresses how the candidate uses technology to plan and implement effective assessment and evaluation strategies

Commentary

The Evaluation Assessment refers to the evaluation of a spectrum of phenomena ranging from student performance, to student use of technology, to district technology plans and instructional practice. Many schools are striving (some succeeding and some faltering) with technology and assessment, particularly as it relates to data-driven decision making. This is an excellent opportunity to assist local schools in this area.

For TF	TF Standard IV should be the focus of this assessment. There are three indicators and four discrete standards. The indicators relate to student learning, instructional practice, and student use of technology. These are three distinct yet interrelated areas involving technology and assessment. A single project that unites these three areas or a related sequence of assessments that combine for one unit assessment would be appropriate here. Also, in most settings this assessment provides an opportunity to integrate other TF standards. One project that has been extremely successful and also helps teachers develop productivity skills is to have them develop a series of Excel templates or Access forms for formative classroom assessments. These templates are targeted to the specific indicators in TF-IV. They would also add context about how to create a culture of assessment.
For TL	This assessment would focus on TL Standard IV. This standard has three indicators and five discrete standards. The focus is on assessing the use of technology for students to learn subject matter, instructional practice, and technology use. As a technology leader, there should be an emphasis on replicable practices, data collection, and analysis techniques.

Assessment 8: VISION ASSESSMENT

Assessment that addresses facilitation of a shared vision for integration of technology and how to foster an environment and culture conducive to the realization of the vision

Commentary

Though neither report states that the target standard is VIII, "Leadership and Vision," this is the standard that would most strongly correlate to this assessment for both TF and TL.

For TF	This assessment can be based on a completely individual assessment or work as a complement to Assessment 4, the assessment related to field experience. If you perform a job-shadowing project in Professional Practice Assessment (4) where the candidate is mentored by school personnel who facilitate the technical integration in schools, the candidate will cover most of the technical content of TF-VIII.E. Work with community partners (TF-VIII.C) dovetails well with the Planning Assessment (2). Field experiences that begin to address most of the discrete standards of TF-VIII.D can be augmented by reflective essays, journals, research projects, or group discussions with appropriate guidelines and assessment criteria. TF-VIII.A involves discussing and evaluating current research and would dovetail with many of the other assessments. The only discrete indicator for TF VIII.B is "Discuss the history of technology use in schools." This would most easily be part of class work that could be appended to most of the Assessments, including number 8.
For TL	The instructions in the Assessment are identical for TL and TF and there are only minor differences in the standards and indicators for TL-VIII and TF-VIII, so please pardon the apparent redundancy with the TF commentary above. This assessment can be based on a completely individual assessment or work as a complement to Assessment 4, the assessment related to field experience. If you perform a job-shadowing project in Professional Practice Assessment (4) where the candidate is mentored by school personnel who facilitate the technical integration in schools, the candidate will cover most of the technical content of TL-VIII.E. Work with community partners (TL-VIII.C) dovetails well with the Planning Assessment (2). Field experiences that begin to address most of the discrete standards of TL-VIII.D can be augmented by reflective essays, journals, research projects, or group discussions with appropriate guidelines and assessment criteria. TL-VIII.A involves discussing and evaluating current research and would dovetail with many of the other assessments. The only discrete indicator for TL-VIII.B is "Describe social and historical foundations of education and how they relate to the use of technology in schools." This would most easily be part of class work that could be appended to most of the Assessments, including number 8.

Sample Assessment

Following is an example of the information you will need to provide in Section II of the report, Assessment and Related Data. You will have to complete an online form that has five sections—two sections need to be filled in (Type of Assessment and When the Assessment Is Administered) and you need to add three attachments (Assessment, Scoring Guides/Criteria, and Data Table). This is an example of Assessment 4, the assessment that demonstrates that the candidates' knowledge, skills, and dispositions are applied effectively in practice. You can view sample assessments from other SPAs online at the NCATE Website (www.ncate.org/institutions/assessmentExamples.asp?ch=90).

Type of Assessment. This assessment is a report about a professional development experience that the candidates must create and implement in a school setting.

When the Assessment Is Administered. This assessment is administered in Introduction to Educational Technology (EDTC 623), a required course for all candidates.

The following attachment samples contain examples of the three attachments you will need to submit:

Attachment 1. The assessment, including the instructions to candidates about the assigned task;

Attachment 2. Scoring guides or criteria used to score candidate responses on the assessment; and

Attachment 3. A table with aggregated results of the assessment providing, where possible, data for each of the most recent three years. Data should be organized according to the categories used in the scoring guide/criteria. Provide the percentage of candidates achieving in each category.

attachment one

SAMPLE ASSESSMENT INSTRUCTIONS

Introduction to Educational Technology

EDTC 623

Spring 2006

Professional Development in Emerging or Underused Technologies Project

OVERVIEW

This project addresses TF standards I.A.1, I.A.2, I.B.1, II.C.2, and VII.C.1.

For this assignment you will choose an easily available emerging or underused technology or feature and create a professional development plan for a group of teachers in a school or district. This group should be from a particular grade or subject and consist of at least eight teachers. You will create and implement the professional development project, then submit a report.

This project has the following components:

- Needs Assessment

- Professional Development Experience (Workshop, Classroom Support, Mentoring Program, or combination)

- Evaluation of Professional Development Efficacy and Reflection

TOPICS

Choose one of the topics below. They are all easily available emerging or underused technologies: Blogs, Audacity Audio Editing Software, Podcasts, RealSlideShow, an RSS Feed Aggregator, Microsoft Movie Maker, Reviewing Toolbar in Word, Advanced Features of Excel (such as Filters, Formulas, and Pivot Tables). The resources and links page has related links and descriptions for all of these applications. Please review them as you consider your choice.

NEEDS ASSESSMENT

Develop a needs assessment for the selected population of teachers whom you will be targeting. This assessment should ascertain their knowledge and use of educational technology in general, and the potential areas where your application could assist them. You should focus on curriculum or classroom areas of interest or trouble (e.g., student research, particular skills). (TF-I.A.1)

attachment one *(Continued)*

PROFESSIONAL DEVELOPMENT EXPERIENCE

Create a Professional Development Experience (Workshop, Workshop Series, Mentoring Program, Classroom Support, or a combination of these techniques) for a target group of teachers on one of the applications.

You should provide technical assistance to the teachers so that they: understand the operations of the technology; model an application of it in education; describe applications aligned with content standards; and assess the efficacy of the professional development. The professional development strategy should be based on adult learning theory. The instruction should include at least seven suggested applications of this technology in the targeted subject and grade; and these suggestions should be aligned with the ISTE NETS (TF-II.C.2 and TF-VII.C.1).

EVALUATION

After the professional development is completed, you should evaluate its efficacy. Survey the participating teachers on the achievement of the goals of the professional development. You should examine the selection of the technology, the design and implementation of the professional development, and the relevance of the integration strategies (TF-I.A.2 and TF-I.B.1).

You will submit a report that includes:

- **Needs Assessment**—surveys and results of needs assessment.

- **Description of Professional Development**—schedule, content, and rationale of the workshop, including the applications of adult learning theory and goals of the professional development. Also include material such as handouts, presentation slides and documentation such as schedules, flyers, and sign-in sheets.

- **Evaluation**—including the number of teachers, date, questions asked, and analysis of responses.

This material should be in one single Word file, with three sections mirroring the topics above. You should insert any presentation slides as .jpg files.

attachment two

SAMPLE SCORING GUIDE

PROJECT COMPONENT	ISTE STANDARD	PERFORMANCE CRITERIA	SCORE AND COMMENTARY
Needs Assessment	TF-I.A.1 Conduct needs assessment to determine baseline data on teachers' knowledge, skills, and understanding of concepts related to technology.	An assessment is given to at least 8 teachers of a particular subject/grade in a school or district. The assessment clearly ascertains the general technical experience and the specific knowledge of the teachers on the topic. Assessment also identifies level and experience with technology integration.	0–3 (20%)
Description of Professional Development Experience	TF-II.C.2 Create professional development lessons integrating technology resources that reflect content standards.	The implementation of the professional development should include at least 8 teachers and be described and documented with dates and sign-in sheets. The professional development experience contains at least 7 suggestions for integration that are aligned with NJ Core Curriculum Content Standards and the ISTE NETS.	0–3 (20%)
	TF-VII.C.1 Design and plan technology professional development at the building/school level utilizing adult learning theory.	The professional development should include a clear overview of the technology and educational applications of the technology specifically targeted to the audience. An analysis of the application of adult learning theory is the description of the workshop. A minimum of two sources is referenced.	0–3 (20%)
Evaluation	TF-I.A.2 Evaluate the effectiveness of modeling used to demonstrate teachers' knowledge, skills, and understanding of concepts related to technology.	The professional development should prominently include a segment where the candidate reflectively models the integration of the technology in education. The assessment should include specific questions on the efficacy of the candidate's modeling of an integration strategy.	0–3 (20%)

attachment two *(Continued)*

Evaluation	TF-I.B.1 Evaluate the effectiveness of modeling appropriate strategies essential to continued growth and development of the understanding of technology operations and concepts.	The professional development should prominently include methods for continuous education and support in the selected technology. This can include Web sites, list-servs, blogs, podcasts, new services, and journals. This aspect of the professional development should be formatively evaluated during the professional development experience and in the final assessment.	0–3 (20%)

Total Score (100%) and Comments

Rubric for Professional Development in Emerging or Underused Technologies Project

3. **Exemplary**—Candidate demonstrates a thorough understanding of the knowledge, skills, and dispositions. Candidate has completed all of the performance criteria in a professional way (well written, well formatted, on time).

2. **Satisfactory**—Candidate demonstrates a clear understanding of the knowledge, skills, and dispositions. Candidate has completed most/all of the performance criteria with some deviation from professional standards.

1. **Emerging**—Candidate demonstrates an incomplete but burgeoning understanding of the knowledge, skills, and dispositions. Candidate has completed some of the performance criteria with some major deviations from professional standards.

0. **Unacceptable**—Candidate demonstrates an incomplete and/or misguided understanding of the knowledge, skills, and dispositions. Candidate has completed little/none of the performance criteria.

RUBRIC SCORE TOTALED	DESCRIPTION	GRADE
13–15	Exemplary	A
12	Satisfactory	B+
9–11	Satisfactory	B
8	Emerging	C+
5–7	Emerging	C
Under 5	Unsatisfactory	F

attachment three
DATA TABLE

AGGREGATED DATA FROM ASSESSMENT 4

The grades were calculated based on the candidate's performance on the criteria for each standard. Each of the five standards was weighed equally to comprise 20% of the total score. Each candidate was scored 0–3 (Unacceptable, Emerging, Satisfactory, Exemplary) on the specific performance criteria for each standard for a total possible score of 15. The scores were totaled and the grades were calculated. The grades were converted to the A–F scale to correlate with the university system. Please note that candidates must maintain a B average to remain in the program. A total of 9 (B) or better was considered passing for this assessment.

RUBRIC SCORE TOTALED	DESCRIPTION	GRADE
13–15	Exemplary	A
12	Satisfactory	B+
9–11	Satisfactory	B
8	Emerging	C+
5–7	Emerging	C
Under 5	Unsatisfactory	F

GRADES AND SCORES FROM ASSESSMENT

Semester		Grade						Percent
		F	C	C+	B	B+	A	Satisfactory or Above
Summer 2005	(N=21)	1	3	2	8	4	3	71.43%
Fall 2005	(N=35)	0	4	3	13	7	8	80.00%
Spring 2006	(N=28)	1	2	2	10	5	8	82.14%

attachment three *(Continued)*
DATA TABLE

PERFORMANCE ON INDIVIDUAL STANDARDS BY SEMESTER

Semester	Standard	Unacceptable		Emerging		Satisfactory		Exemplary	
Summer 2005 (N=21)	I.A.1	2	9.52%	3	14.29%	7	33.33%	9	42.86%
	I.A.2	2	9.52%	4	19.05%	3	14.29%	12	57.14%
	II.B.1	2	9.52%	6	28.57%	8	38.10%	5	23.81%
	II.C.2	2	9.52%	5	23.81%	8	38.10%	6	28.57%
	VII.C.1	2	9.52%	5	23.81%	6	28.57%	8	38.10%
Fall 2005 (N=35)	I.A.1	1	2.86%	3	8.57%	12	34.29%	19	54.29%
	I.A.2	2	5.71%	1	2.86%	10	28.57%	22	62.86%
	I.B.1	1	2.86%	4	11.43%	10	28.57%	20	57.14%
	II.C.2	1	2.86%	2	5.71%	15	42.86%	17	48.57%
	VII.C.1	1	2.86%	5	14.29%	13	37.14%	16	45.71%
Spring 2006 (N=28)	I.A.1	2	7.14%	5	17.86%	7	25.00%	14	50.00%
	I.A.2	1	3.57%	3	10.71%	6	21.43%	18	64.29%
	I.B.1	2	7.14%	5	17.86%	7	25.00%	14	50.00%
	II.C.2	2	7.14%	2	7.14%	10	35.71%	14	50.00%
	VII.C.1	2	7.14%	6	21.43%	9	32.14%	11	39.29%

attachment three *(Continued)*

DATA TABLE

AGGREGATED CANDIDATE PERFORMANCE BY STANDARD

Standard	Semester	Unacceptable		Emerging		Satisfactory		Exemplary	
I.A.1	Summer 2005 *(N=21)*	2	9.52%	3	14.29%	7	33.33%	9	42.86%
	Fall 2005 *(N=35)*	1	2.86%	3	8.57%	12	34.29%	19	54.29%
	Spring 2006 *(N=28)*	2	7.14%	5	17.86%	7	25.00%	14	50.00%
Totals for Standard *(N=84)*		5	5.95%	11	13.10%	26	30.95%	42	50.00%
I.A.2	Summer 2005 *(N=21)*	2	9.52%	4	19.05%	3	14.29%	12	57.14%
	Fall 2005 *(N=35)*	2	5.71%	1	2.86%	10	28.57%	22	62.86%
	Spring 2006 *(N=28)*	1	3.57%	3	10.71%	6	21.43%	18	64.29%
Totals for Standard *(N=84)*		5	5.95%	8	9.52%	19	22.62%	52	61.90%
I.B.1	Summer 2005 *(N=21)*	2	9.52%	6	28.57%	8	38.10%	5	23.81%
	Fall 2005 *(N=35)*	1	2.86%	4	11.43%	10	28.57%	20	57.14%
	Spring 2006 *(N=28)*	2	7.14%	5	17.86%	7	25.00%	14	50.00%
Totals for Standard *(N=84)*		5	5.95%	15	17.86%	25	29.76%	39	46.43%
II.C.2	Summer 2005 *(N=21)*	2	9.52%	5	23.81%	8	38.10%	6	28.57%
	Fall 2005 *(N=35)*	1	2.86%	2	5.71%	15	42.86%	17	48.57%
	Spring 2006 *(N=28)*	2	7.14%	2	7.14%	10	35.71%	14	50.00%
Totals for Standard *(N=84)*		5	5.95%	9	10.71%	33	39.29%	37	44.05%

Teachers as Technology Leaders

attachment three *(Continued)*

DATA TABLE

AGGREGATED CANDIDATE PERFORMANCE BY STANDARD

Standard	Semester	Unacceptable		Emerging		Satisfactory		Exemplary	
VII.C.1	Summer 2005 *(N=21)*	2	9.52%	5	23.81%	6	28.57%	8	38.10%
	Fall 2005 *(N=35)*	1	2.86%	5	14.29%	13	37.14%	16	45.71%
	Spring 2006 *(N=28)*	2	7.14%	6	21.43%	9	32.14%	11	39.29%
Totals for Standard *(N=84)*		5	5.95%	16	19.05%	28	33.33%	35	41.67%

Technology Used to Assess the Standards

In general, technology is not required for program assessment, but it can help... a lot. Considering that both the TF and the TL Standard IV is Assessment and Evaluation and Standard V is Productivity and Professional Practice, we would strongly recommend its use for your assessment system. If you are going to use a technologically-based assessment system, there are two general directions in which you can go—dedicated assessment systems or generic tools.

There are some general trends and some specific issues in higher education of which you should be aware. For example, there are more options in the P–12 environment for assessment systems and dedicated technological tools for data-driven decision making (DDDM). The large P–12 market has encouraged a myriad of such systems. McLeod (2005) has an excellent overview of technology assessment systems for P–12 schools and DDDM. Though much of the dedicated software is specific to the P–12 curriculum, McLeod's discussion of using products such as Excel and Access for creating a classroom-centered culture of assessment and DDDM are extremely applicable to higher education.

Many Units employ online assessment systems or electronic portfolios in their data collection. The current state of electronic portfolios in teacher education programs is an evolution of earlier trends in the use of paper portfolios. Portfolios began as an alternative way to assess and showcase student work and have now become a standard practice for most institutions. It is estimated that 90% of teacher preparation programs use some form of portfolio system for assessing candidates (Salzman et al, 2002). Electronic portfolios offer institutions, students, and faculty new opportunities to learn, reflect, and showcase their work. Cambridge (2001) provides a thorough overview of the use of electronic portfolios in higher education.

The popularity of electronic portfolios over the last few years has coincided with and been encouraged by the DDDM requirements of accreditation. The response of commercial vendors to the needs of accreditation makes it important to distinguish between electronic portfolios and online assessment systems. Though there are many vendors who promote their products as electronic portfolio systems, these systems are more accurately termed online assessment systems (Barrett, 2004). The procedures and tools of these systems assist in the correlation and aggregation of data and not the more individualistic and creative attributes associated with electronic or paper portfolios. LiveText, Chalk and Wire, and Task Stream are three vendors of online assessment systems. Many of these systems were originally designed to be used as instructional tools in P–12 schools but evolved to address the assessment and accreditation needs of programs and schools of education. They are popular technologies for collecting and aggregating program assessment data. Our program researched and piloted such a system and decided that a system based on common applications, Excel and Access would suit our needs better. We will describe our experiences in more detail later in this chapter.

Many institutions use Learning Management Systems (LMS) such as WebCT and Blackboard or open source LMSs such as Moodle or Plone. All of these systems have assessment procedures that can be tailored to program assessment. The two largest commercial systems, LMSs, WebCT and Blackboard (which recently merged), are currently developing assessment tools aimed at accreditation. WebCT's Quality Vista

Project (WebCT, 2005) aims to "help colleges and universities improve education by analyzing the student performance data" and Blackboard's Caliper initiative is a "product development effort aimed at addressing the growing assessment and evaluation needs of educators in both traditional and e-Learning programs" (*In practice*, 2005). Although both of these specific assessment projects are in their beginning stages, the current assessment systems of most LMSs can be adapted to address your data collection needs.

While some of our data was collected through our LMS, the central collection and aggregation method utilized Microsoft Access and Excel. Using these common tools has several advantages. There is no extra software to be purchased and little additional technical training for most faculty members. While you will need a faculty member or assessment coordinator to lead the project, the use of generic tools facilitates greater faculty involvement in the process.

We recommend an Excel spreadsheet for each assessment. You can create a template for each assessment and enter candidate performance on each rubric item. For example, based on Assessment 4, the Professional Practice Assessment, to address 5 of the 78 indicators, you can create columns for each standard and key in the scores for each candidate. Data entry, aggregation, and calculation become much easier once you develop the design. One important distinction is that ISTE only requires data on the indicator. To provide a comprehensive and detailed view of the process, we went to the discrete indicator level. Though this is not required by ISTE for either the TF or the TL report, it is useful because the discrete indicators have the accompanying rubrics for the development of the candidate assessments.

FIGURE 1 ■ Example of Excel spreadsheet used to aggregate program assessment data.

B	C	D	E	F	G	H
			Assessment 4			
				Needs Assessment	Professional	Development
Student ID	First Name	Last Name	Semester	TF-1.A.1	TF-1.A.2	TF-7.C.1
44567	Archie	Bunker	Summer 05	3	3	2
46367	Edith	Bunker	Summer 05	3	3	3
43543	George	Castanza	Summer 05	2	3	2
12461	Diane	Chambers	Summer 05	1	1	1
55432	J.R.	Ewing	Summer 05	3	3	3
67589	Lou	Grant	Summer 05	3	3	3
23134	Laura	Ingalls	Summer 05	3	3	3
22460	Louise	Jefferson	Summer 05	3	3	2
13452	Michael	Keaton	Summer 05	2	2	1
36744	Alice	Kramden	Summer 05	1	1	1
31456	Cosmo	Kramer	Summer 05	2	3	2
11135	George	Lopez	Summer 05	2	2	2
89009	Oscar	Madison	Summer 05	0	0	0
86432	Thomas	Magnum	Summer 05	3	2	3
23154	Sam	Malone	Summer 05	3	3	3
56473	Rhoda	Morgenstern	Summer 05	2	2	2
21231	Les	Nessman	Summer 05	3	3	3
65432	Trixie	Norton	Summer 05	1	1	1
12342	Mel	Sharples	Summer 05	3	3	3
33268	Felix	Unger	Summer 05	0	0	0
75432	J.J.	Walker	Summer 05	2	3	2

Once the template is created, you can add candidates; sort and filter by candidate, semester, or rubric item; and import scores from Access, another Excel sheet, or an LMS as tab-delimited data. If you have a large number of candidates, you can use tools such as pivot tables to aggregate performance data. You can simplify the data entry process for less experienced Excel users by improving the formatting, locking cells, freezing panes, and creating validation lists of acceptable inputs. It takes some planning, a small piloting period, and continuous modification. However, it has been our experience that it is in some ways easier and more user-friendly than commercial online assessment systems. The most useful part of the program is that you can aggregate and disaggregate data by student, semester, and standard and create formulas that proportionally weight your scores to reflect a fair and credible assessment process.

This can also be done in Microsoft Access, which gives you more flexibility in the interface for input and in the generation of reports. Furthermore, if your department and your institution have been consistent in using candidate IDs or another constant in compiling candidate information, data can be imported and exported from other databases. The candidate ID will act as the primary key to merge and create relationships among these various data sources. Using a candidate ID consistently will turn it into the lynchpin of working efficiently and effectively with your data and aggregating your assessments in Access. If you are choosing between Excel and Access you should consider the size of your program (Access is better with larger databases), the technical level of your faculty and staff, and the number of people who will be inputting and manipulating data (Excel is better known and more easily shared).

Summary

Your assessment system should not be looked at as preparation for ISTE accreditation or an NCATE visit, but as an effective way to monitor and improve your program. As you gather and analyze the data, you will find your hunches validated as well as some of your assumptions contradicted. Just as important are the reflection and collaboration in creating, maintaining, and improving your system. Writing the report is not the end of your job, but a still picture of an ongoing journey.

chapter eight
Writing the Report

The format of the TF and the TL reports are almost identical. There are five parts to each of the forms—the "Program Report for the Preparation of Technology Facilitation Teachers" (which we will refer to as the TF Report) and the "Program Report for the Preparation of Technology Leaders" (which we will refer to as the TL Report). The major distinction is the standards that each report should address. These forms can be found at the NCATE Web site and the ISTE Web site:

NCATE—Public—Standards (www.ncate.org/public/programStandards.asp)

NETS: National Council for Accreditation of Teacher Education (http://cnets.iste.org/ncate/)

At the time of publication, the report form at the NCATE Web site was a more current, revised version.

There are five major parts of both reports:

I. Contextual Information

II. Assessments and Related Data

III. Standards Assessment Chart

IV. Evidence of Meeting Standards

V. Use of Assessment Results to Improve Candidate and Program Performance

There is a sixth section only for programs that are being resubmitted after initially not meeting all of the standards in an original application. Aside from the first section, Contextual Information, all of the other four sections are based on the eight program assessments previously discussed.

These eight assessments are the fundamental aspects of your assessment system and should address the TF or the TL standards. The fact that there are eight required assessments and eight TF and TL standards is somewhat coincidental and does not imply that there should be a one-to-one correspondence between assessment and standard. Indeed, one assessment may apply to multiple ISTE standards. It has been our experience that when using the principles of learner-centered pedagogy and authentic assessment techniques, an exclusive correlation between a single standard and assessment could become contrived and counterintuitive.

The requirements outlined for accreditation in the reports have substantially changed from previous versions and are now consistent with the requirements and format of the reports from other Specialty Professional Associations (SPAs) like the National Association for the Education of Young Children, the International Reading Association, and the National Council of Teachers of Mathematics.

This move to consistency was initiated by NCATE. Institutions applying for NCATE accreditation need to satisfy the six NCATE standards (cited in Chapter 4). An institution addresses a part of the first standard, Content Knowledge, when the individual departments and programs successfully achieve their SPAs' accreditation. NCATE accreditation requires the successful accreditation of departments and programs by their SPAs.

The crux of the report for TF or TL accreditation is the eight assessments that target the 33 indicators of the eight standards. To implement these eight assessments there are two general courses of action and a spectrum of options between them. One is that you use existing assessments that fit the eight prescribed ISTE assessments, and the other is to create an original assessment based on the eight ISTE assessments. You will probably begin by correlating your existing courses and assessments to the ISTE assessments, modifying these assessments to match the eight ISTE assessments and address the standards, then possibly creating some new ones.

Report Overview

Writing the report can be a successful experience when faculty welcome the process and do not see it as a procedure of compliance. This might sound unrealistic, especially if you have an impending deadline; however, an earnest effort to develop an assessment system will come through in the report. This sense of credibility is extremely important for the entire process. We found it essential to build a commitment to the assessment process and the value of program improvement—this means dedicating time and resources. It also means having a safe place to share ideas, challenges, and reluctances.

There are some broader values of evaluation that should guide the reporting process and assessment system. Your system should consider a variety of assessments (e.g., papers, exams, observations, projects, interviews, and portfolios). You should be ready to plan backwards. This means that you need to base assignments and rubrics on the TF or the TL standards and your Unit's conceptual framework. Collaboration is another key component of a successful assessment system. Developing and improving the assessment system and writing the report provide opportunities to unite the vision of the department to the daily practices of your faculty and candidates. You need to be committed to data-driven improvements of your program. Like many of the elements of the TF or the TL accreditation, it is not only required for the report, but it is also a helpful practice in general. Many times your data will verify your intuitions; other times the data will make you look at your assumptions in a different way.

It is helpful if you look at the accreditation process as an excellent opportunity to upgrade your courses and programs. These standards represent a current and broad consideration of the field of educational technology. It has been our experience that examining the standards can be a catalyst for departments to reinvigorate their work. Preparing the accreditation report and developing the assessment system should be a collaborative effort—input from the stakeholders listed in Chapter 4, candidates, P–12 administrators, as well as a literature reviews are essential.

Section I. Contextual Information

The first section of the report is the context. This section consists of five parts and three attachments. The five parts should not exceed six pages.

1. **Descriptions of any state or institutional policies that may influence the application of ISTE standards.** This can include such guidelines as union regulations regarding teaching loads, course requirements from the Unit, joint major requirements, state licensing policies, specialty certificates, interdisciplinary programs, service learning components, and externship requirements of the Unit.

2. **Description of the field and clinical experiences required for the program, including the number of hours for early field experiences and the number of hours/weeks.** These programs must include field experiences in which candidates are working with schools and teachers. This type of work is embedded throughout the TF and the TL standards and should be considered field experience. In this section you would describe these experiences as they are structured within individual courses.

3. **Description of the criteria for admission, retention, and exit from the program, including required GPAs and minimum grade requirements for the content courses accepted by the program.** This section will describe the policies from your institution, Unit, and program. For example, we have general admission requirements from our University; the College of Education has additional requirements; and the Department has an added layer of policies for entry, retention, and graduation.

4. **Description of the relationship of the program to the Unit's conceptual framework.** The conceptual framework is the guiding light of your Unit. In many cases, either as a preparation for an NCATE visit or as a general practice, course syllabi are

aligned to the conceptual framework. You might want to include these correlations or generally review the conceptual framework and describe how your program advances specific values or goals of the conceptual framework.

5. **Indication of whether the program has a unique set of program assessments and the relationship of the program's assessments to the Unit's assessment system.** This information "should clarify how the key assessments used in the program are derived from and informed by the assessment system that the Unit will address under NCATE Standard 2" (TL Report, 2005; TF Report, 2005). In many instances several of these eight assessments or other assessments are part of the Unit's Assessment System. In our program we have three assessments (entry, midpoint, and exit) that are used for the Unit assessment; one of these is also one of our eight assessments for this reporting system. We also administer a survey and complete a questionnaire for each candidate at entry, midpoint, and exit from the program. This survey is correlated to our conceptual framework and the data is used for our own program improvement and for the Unit to aggregate, analyze, and act upon.

ATTACHMENTS

A program of study that outlines the courses and experiences required for candidates to complete the program.

1. The first attachment is the program of study that outlines the courses and experiences required for candidates to complete the program. The program of study must include course titles. (This information may be provided as an attachment from the institution's catalog or as a candidate advisement sheet.) Only assessment related to required courses are considered as evidence. Assessment data from elective courses need not be submitted as evidence because there is no assurance that all candidates enroll in that course.

2. The second attachment is a chart with the number of candidates and completers. (A table is provided for this at the end of the current TF and TL reports.)

3. The third attachment is a chart of program faculty expertise and experience. (A table is provided for this at the end of the current TF and TL reports.) As a preparation, you should ensure that your entire faculty, adjuncts included, has their vitas updated.

Section II. Assessments and Related Data

Sections II, III, and IV are based on the data from your assessment system. For Section II, Assessments and Related Data, you need to specify the type or form of the assessment (portfolio, essay, exam, observation, etc.) and when it is administered in the program (admission to the program, midpoint courses, before field experience).

FIGURE 2 ■ Excerpt from Section II, Assessments and Related Data.

NAME OF ASSESSMENT	TYPE OR FORM OF ASSESSMENT	WHEN THE ASSESSMENT IS ADMINISTERED
1. Program entry-level benchmark, or licensure tests, or professional examinations of content knowledge		
2. Assessment of content knowledge in the field of Educational Technology Leadership		
3. Assessment that demonstrates candidates can collaborate effectively; plan, design, and model effective learning environments; and plan and implement professional experiences required of a technology leader		
4. Assessment that demonstrates candidates' knowledge, skills, and dispositions are applied effectively in practice		
5. Assessment that demonstrates the candidate models, designs, and disseminates methods and strategies in technology that enhance student learning		
6. Assessment that demonstrates the candidate understands and can develop programs that address the social, legal and ethical issues related to technology within the district/region/state		
7. Assessment that addresses how the candidate uses technology to plan and implement effective assessment and evaluation strategies		
8. Assessment that addresses facilitation of a shared vision for integration of technology and how to foster an environment and culture conducive to the realization of the vision		

Section III. Standards Assessment Chart

Section III of the report is the Standards Assessment Chart. This chart asks you to correlate the assessments from Section II to the ISTE Standard.

FIGURE 3 ■ Excerpt from Section III, Standards Assessment Chart.

ISTE STANDARD	APPLICABLE ASSESSMENTS FROM SECTION II
TL-I. Technology Operations and Concepts. Educational technology leaders demonstrate an advanced understanding of technology operations and concepts. Educational technology leaders:	
A. Demonstrate knowledge, skills, and understanding of concepts related to technology (as described in the ISTE National Education Technology Standards for Teachers).	
1. Identify and evaluate components needed for the continual growth of knowledge, skills, and understanding of concepts related to technology.	☐ #1 ☐ #2 ☐ #3 ☐ #4 ☐ #5 ☐ #6 ☐ #7 ☐ #8
2. Offer a variety of professional development opportunities that facilitate the ongoing development of knowledge, skills, and understanding of concepts related to technology.	
B. Demonstrate continual growth in technology knowledge and skills to stay abreast of current and emerging technologies.	
1. Offer a variety of professional development opportunities that facilitate the continued growth and development of the understanding of technology operations and concepts.	☐ #1 ☐ #2 ☐ #3 ☐ #4 ☐ #5 ☐ #6 ☐ #7 ☐ #8

When you fill out this section, you need to correlate the standards to the assessments in your system. This section is extremely important because, as noted in the previous chapter, it will inform the way you develop your assessments, collect assessment data, and report that data. Please notice that you are accountable for addressing the lettered indicator, e.g., TL-I.A, not the discrete standard, e.g., TL-I.A.1. This simplifies the reporting process but does complicate the assessment process somewhat. The discrete indicators are guidelines for your report. However, when developing student assessments you should focus on the discrete indicator. There is more precise information on the skills that you will be assessing and ISTE provides rubrics for the discrete indicator. There are no specific rubrics to guide you in assessing the indicator.

Section IV. Evidence of Meeting Standards

The previous section reviewed the assessments in detail. Section IV is a comprehensive look at each of the assessments. For each of the eight assessments you must write: 1) a brief description of the assessment and its use in the program—this can be as brief as one sentence; 2) the alignment of the assessment with the specific standard and indictor from Section III; 3) a brief analysis of the data findings; and 4) an interpretation of how that data provides evidence for meeting the standards. Each of these eight descriptions is limited to two pages. **An example is provided below.** You must also provide: (a) an attachment of the assessment tool or description of the assignment, (b) the scoring guide for the assessment, and (c) the aggregate candidate data derived for the assessment.

EXAMPLE: *Assessment 6*

1. This assessment is the Reflective Mentoring Assignment given to the students in Seminar: Current Issues and Trends in Educational Technology, a required course taken during the middle of the program and designated as a Midpoint indicator. In the Reflective Mentoring Assignment candidates mentor 5 to 7 teachers in:

    ■ technology for curricular integration

    ■ applications of assistive technology

    ■ technology to support cultural and linguistic differences

    ■ the social, legal, and ethical use of technology

    Concurrent with recording their mentoring experiences, candidates must record their own experiences integrating technology in their teaching and work. This project uses reflective practice for candidates to draw on their own experiences in specific areas of technology and to share these experiences with teachers whom they are mentoring.

    This project runs for the entire course and is submitted and scored at the end of the semester. However, there are weekly discussions online and face-to-face to give candidates formative feedback and guidance on their work. Detailed instructions, examples from past courses and the scoring rubric are provided to candidates.

2. The final product is the candidates' journal with an analysis of how they addressed each of the standards. The scoring rubric looks at both the journal entries and the analysis and examines the candidates' work in their own teaching and work with the teachers. There have been a few modifications of this project for candidates who were not teaching at the time. These modifications were reviewed by the department chair and another faculty member.

    The project and assessment is correlated to discrete standards of TF-III.B.1, II.A.3, VI.B.1, VI.B.2, VI.C.1, VI.D.1, V.A.2, VI.A.1, VI.A.2, and VI.E.1, and indicators for Section III of this report of TF-III.B, II.A, VI.B, VI.B, VI.C, VI.D, V.A, VI.A, VI.A, and VI.E.

EXAMPLE: *Assessment 6*

Below is the data from our rubric for three years of administering the assessment. During this time, 185 candidates have completed the course. During the three years there have been a few modifications in the instructions to clarify the requirements and correlation to the standards. After the first year one standard was eliminated: TF-II.D.1—Provide teachers with options for the management of technology resources within the context of learning activities. Though teachers did this successfully, it seemed disconnected from the other objectives of the mentoring and was better taught and assessed in another project.

3. See Table 5 below for examples of a brief summary of data findings for Section IV, Evidence of Meeting Standards.

TABLE 5 ■ Examples of A Brief Summary of Data Findings for Section IV, Evidence of Meeting Standards.

Standard	Unacceptable	Emerging	Satisfactory	Exemplary	Met Standard*
III.B.1	3.24%	10.27%	42.16%	44.86%	87.03%
II.A.3	2.70%	6.49%	48.65%	42.70%	91.35%
VI.B.1	2.70%	12.97%	32.43%	52.43%	84.86%
VI.B.2	2.70%	12.97%	42.16%	42.70%	84.86%
VI.C.1	3.78%	12.43%	31.89%	52.43%	84.32%
VI.D.1	3.24%	9.73%	21.08%	66.49%	87.57%
V.A.2	2.70%	5.41%	29.73%	62.70%	92.43%
VI.A.1	2.70%	10.81%	22.16%	64.86%	87.03%
VI.A.2	3.24%	16.22%	24.32%	56.76%	81.08%
VI.E.1	2.70%	5.95%	21.08%	70.81%	91.89%

(Satisfactory and Exemplary Combined)

4. The standards were met substantively in this project and assessment. For each targeted standard, more than 80% of our candidates did work that was satisfactory or exemplary. As we collected data for the three years, we did notice an initial weakness in TF-VI.A.2—Assist others in summarizing copyright laws related to use of images, music, video, and other digital resources in varying formats. The first year of data showed only 66% of the students demonstrating work that was satisfactory or exemplary. We analyzed the student work and the scope and sequence of the assignments as assessments and clarified both the instructional content and directions for that element of the reflective journal.

Section V. Use of Assessment Results to Improve Candidate and Program Performance

Section V requires that you describe changes in the program based on the data from the assessments. These can be changes that were already implemented, are currently employed, or changes you plan to put into action. The analysis of the data should not be directly related to the assessments but should be organized by overriding principles. You need to describe the process of the data analysis and interpretation by the faculty and other stakeholders. You need to describe the steps taken or planned to improve candidate and program performance.

These decisions should be organized around: 1) content knowledge; 2) pedagogical and professional knowledge, skills and dispositions; and 3) effects on student learning on creative environments that support learning. For example, a consistent theme in our data was that candidates were challenged by standards related to leadership knowledge, primarily the knowledge involved in troubleshooting and maintaining network-wide software and hardware. We revised an existing elective course and made it a required course. This new requisite course contained the content that candidates needed.

Section VI. For Revised Reports Only

In this section you need to describe the changes in your program and how you addressed the standards that were not met in your original report. In most cases you will not be asked to re-submit the entire report, only the revised material or new assessments for standards that were originally designated as unmet by reviewers (NCATE, 2004).

The Review Process and Guidelines on Decisions

After your report is submitted, ISTE will assign a team of three reviewers to read it. These reviewers have been trained in the TF and the TL standards by ISTE and have been pre-selected to avoid potential conflicts of interest. One team member will be the lead reviewer. The resolution and accreditation decision will be determined by a consensus of the team and reported by the lead reviewer. If the team does not reach a consensus, the report will be reviewed by an ISTE Audit Committee, which will make the final accreditation decision. These are the procedures prescribed by NCATE for all SPAs (NCATE, 2006).

There are four possible decisions that ISTE can make regarding the accreditation of your program. These decisions are consistent among all SPAs affiliated with NCATE.

Your program can be *nationally recognized*. This can happen even if some criteria are not met and there is need for improvement. This accreditation remains in effect until the next NCATE visit and application for accreditation.

Your program can be *nationally recognized, with conditions*. This would happen if your assessment system was sound—well implemented and aligned to SPA standards—but there was insufficient data collected from it. You would then have 18 months to remove the conditions by supplying the required data. If you fail to do so, then your program would revert to non-accredited status.

ISTE can also decide to *defer the decision, more information required*. This decision occurs if there are missing documents or if there is a request for clarification. In this case the reviewers are not able to conduct a valid review and reach a decision because they have inadequate information. Your program has approximately two months to supply the required information. After the information is supplied, the program can be *nationally recognized* or *nationally recognized with conditions* or *not nationally recognized*.

If the information is not provided or is unsatisfactory, your program will be *not nationally recognized*. A program is *not nationally recognized* if it has failed to provide satisfactory additional information after being conditionally recognized or having the decision deferred. Or this can be the initial decision if there are serious or fundamental problems with the assessment system or data.

If your program is not nationally recognized you can submit a revised or new program report within 18 months. If your program is initially not recognized by ISTE, the NCATE BOE team automatically cites your program in Areas for Improvement in their report on the Unit.

Summary

By now we hope that you see that accreditation is an on-going process. Unit III provided the "nuts and bolts" to guide you through the Technology Facilitation process. In Unit IV we will look at future trends in the Technology Facilitation and the Technology Leadership fields, viewed through the eight TF and TL standards.

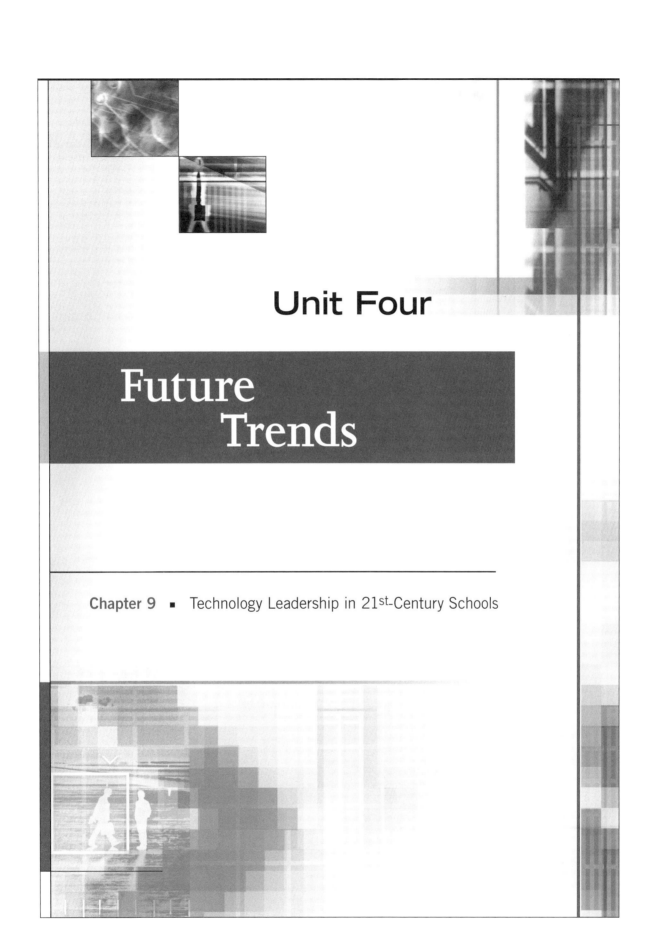

Unit Four

Future Trends

Chapter 9 ■ Technology Leadership in 21st-Century Schools

Technology Leadership in 21st-Century Schools

There are basic assumptions that we can make about the impact of technologies on student learning based on what we have seen in the past and what is going on in the present. Advances in both pedagogy and information technologies have the potential to transform education in ways that were previously unimaginable. The technologies we know now can and will change and evolve at an increasingly rapid rate. Simply consider the progression of the Internet over the last 20 years. The term the "World Wide Web" was only founded in 1990. In addition, the power and speed of today's technologies have been estimated to double every 18 months. The price of this technology, at the same time, declines approximately 35% a year relative to the power. With this rapid growth, there is potential for exciting innovations in education.

Today, there are technologies that may transform education over the next five years. However, if educational practices continue to operate in the same old paradigm, adding technology to the curriculum without pedagogical underpinnings and proper professional development, then outcomes will be less beneficial and much less possible. Teacher-mediated classrooms do not foster technology-rich learning. If American education seeks to improve teaching and learning, educators have at their disposal an arsenal of pedagogically potent new educational technology capabilities.

The technology facilitators' and leaders' roles are to make those in the schools aware of these new tools and then facilitate their integration into the curriculum. Hiring the right experts to assist and support teachers in integrating technology into their daily lesson plans is a crucial step in the right direction.

There are several stakeholders who influence future trends in technology in schools. The government has the power to mandate bills and provide funding for technology, such as the U.S. Department of Education's funded Preparations for Today's Teachers to Use Technology (PT³) program or the No Child Left Behind Act (NCLB). States have the majority of the responsibility to educate their children. This affects of curriculum, funding, and technology priorities of schools in the United States. Administrators have control of the budgets to purchase technology and the authority to request its use in the schools. Parents and the community influence the schools to include more state-of-the-art technology in the classrooms. The technology manufacturers themselves have the responsibility to create and develop software and hardware that would be beneficial in education. Students have the desire and the will to use the tools on a daily basis and, ultimately, teachers are the agents by which all will be delivered. Technology facilitators and technology leaders shoulder the responsibility to keep abreast of current trends and future prospects, mediating between all of the stakeholders. They are the proponents of technology who constantly look for new ideas and information to share with the teachers in their schools. In return, they must be able to teach technology skills as well as understand ways to utilize technology to support instructional goals.

How can these experts predict future trends in educational technology? To judge the potential of technology in the schools, one need only look at the present state and future potential of technology use in relation to the TF and the TL standards:

I.   Technology Operations and Concepts

II.   Planning and Designing Learning Environments and Experiences

III.   Teaching, Learning, and the Curriculum

IV.   Assessment and Evaluation

V.   Productivity and Professional Practice

VI.   Social, Ethical, Legal, and Human Issues

VII.   Procedures, Policies, Planning, and Budgeting for Technology Environments

VIII.   Leadership and Vision

I. Technology Operations and Concepts

Data collected in 2002 by the National Center for Education Statistics and reported in *The Condition of Education 2002* show a serious disengagement between the so-called Millennials and their schools. Millennials are defined by different people in different ways but usually the term refers to children and teenagers born after 1981. They are the current generation of children who are growing up wired and who spend more time on the Internet than watching television. Of this generation, only 28% of 12th-grade high school students believe that school work is meaningful; 21% believe that their courses are interesting; and a mere 39% believe that school work will have any bearing on their success in later life (Wirt, et al., 2002).

The Internet began during the early childhood of the oldest Millennials; they have grown up understanding how it works. Millennials are remarkably computer savvy and familiar with the newest technology operations and concepts and spend much of their free time playing computer or video games, either together in their bedrooms or separated by thousands of miles online.

In 2004, more than 55,000 Millennials answered the question: "What would you like to see invented that you think will help kids learn in the future?" The four most common themes were:

■ Digital Devices

■ Access to Computers and the Internet

■ Intelligent Tutor/Helper

■ Ways to Learn and Complete School Work Using Technology
(Visions 2020.2, 2005)

Digital Devices

Today's students have grown up with digital devices integrated into their everyday lives. Computers, the Internet, instant messaging, cell phones, e-mail and mp3 players have become second nature (much in the same way that televisions, answering machines, and VCRs are common devices used by their parents). The NetDay 2005 Visions 2020.2 report cites that 94% of students ages 12–17 acknowledge that they use the Internet to do research for school assignments, with only a quarter of these students using traditional sources like magazines and books from a library.

While digital devices are commonly utilized, there are ways in which they can be improved. The most requested change by the Millenials is a digital convergence of the capabilities of many devices into one multifunctional, interactive digital device—a smaller handheld computer/cell phone combination to replace textbooks and to be used for homework, perhaps voice-activated with the power to be a digital organizer, planner, video phone, electronic dictionary, digital camera, calculator, DVD player, CD/mp3 player, TV, printer, tape recorder, and the list goes on!

If this request becomes a reality, and we have no reason not to believe it will, handheld computers will be able to calculate exponentially faster than the laptops of today. They will become digital assistants, allowing everything from multimedia production to virtual data collection to multifunctional communication devices.

Many of us can remember the first mainframe computers filling an entire office, requiring four skilled technicians to operate, and being fed data by inserting punch cards. These mammoths boasted a massive eight megabytes of storage capacity. Since the inception of the personal computer in 1981, the natural progression of technology has equipped us with the more portable laptop computers we enjoy today. These laptops are now being replaced by the personal digitized assistant (PDA) or hand-held computer. Predicted by Daggett (2005), in the near future Smart Personal Object Technology (SPOT) will become the next trend. SPOT will be integrated in our watches, essentially functioning as a PC, with the user projecting the image of both a screen and keyboard from the SPOT unit onto a tabletop or piece of paper and working as if using a regular PC and keyboard.

Access to Computers and the Internet

Access is fundamental to opportunity. Reports indicate that American students have growing access to and use of computers and the Internet. Following in this trend, in 2002, 99% of public schools in the United States had access to the Internet (Visions 2020.2, 2005). The use of computers is growing both in the homes and in the schools. The wish of today's Millenials, however, is a computer for every student. This access must be convenient and affordable. It must be located where the learner needs it—in the home, in school, or on the road. In addition to personal computing power, these students also desire faster computers, faster Internet access, wireless technologies, kid-friendly Internet, 24/7 access to school networks from home, and collaborative plat-forms—peer-to-peer, student-to-teacher, and student-to-parent.

How would this access affect the learning environment? Perhaps wireless workstations would allow students to collaborate, mentor, and work with experts in the field of their study. Communication would happen anywhere and at anytime. Concepts could be revisited with the ability to send and receive video and audio in real time. Access also implies content that is child-friendly. Much of the Internet today is created for adults. Content and applications that have meaning and value for students would be readily available, allowing for innovative content that can be brought into the classroom and beyond.

Intelligent Tutor/Helper

The Millenials are greatly interested in an intelligent tutor. This type of expert resource is currently growing within the online library community, allowing for 24/7 expert help. This type of Web-based tutoring is also available at several Web sites, offering virtual tutors or online experts. The gist of this technology is a virtual mentor that can be accessed anytime. Thus, the future of educational technology may be connecting people—teachers, students, parents, human tutors, counselors and experts—in a variety of automated help systems for addressing routine questions as well as a worldwide network for real-time dialogue.

In addition, computers may have the power to detect when a student is having difficulties and adjust accordingly, whether offering further explanation, an alternate perspective of the problem, or support resources. Intelligent tutors may also adjust to the learning styles of the student and offer resources and assessments that are more helpful for that individual learning style. Notification of a student's progress may be reported by the computer to the teacher and/or parent.

Ways to Learn and Complete School Work Using Technology

The Millenials are using technology in their everyday lives—e-mailing relatives, sharing online photo albums, chatting with friends via instant messaging, downloading music to their mp3 players, surfing the Web for information and much more. The only environment where technology is not a part of their everyday lives is in their schools. Students would thrive in a hardware-and-software-enabled learning process, with hands-on exploration of concepts, simulated laboratories, e-books, virtual collaboration, and digital management and storage solutions.

The creation of a tele-immersive environment for teaching and learning would greatly enhance the motivation for students and teachers alike. Individual learning styles and disabilities would be accommodated and greater communication among students, parents, teachers and tutors would be possible and encouraged. This type of a three-dimensional space would allow for self-paced learning for students to reach their full potential. Students working in such sophisticated environments would understand the underlying principles of the facts they are studying. Knowledge would become scaffolded and shared, rather than the gathering of isolated facts.

II. Planning and Designing Learning Environments and Experiences

There are currently powerful, low-cost tools that can make learning environments and experiences more engaging and knowledge more accessible. For example, digital video is being integrated by more than 1,000,000 teachers through Discovery Education's *unitedstreaming* program. American education need not be reinvented; it simply needs to explore the new tools that are currently available. Technology facilitators and leaders, keeping informed of these tools, are poised to create the technology-rich learning environments of the future.

More than two-thirds of all public schools have broadband or high-speed access to the Internet. More than 40% of all homes in the United States also have high-speed access. With better data packet handling capabilities, online learning takes place seamlessly—materials download instantly, communication is in real-time, and the Internet responds quickly and dependably. The new Internet2 project will mean greater broadband access. Led by more than 200 U.S. universities, working with industry and government, Internet2 develops and deploys advanced network applications and technologies for research and higher education, accelerating the creation of tomorrow's Internet. In addition, an unprepossessing technology called Wi-Fi (wireless fidelity) transmits high-speed Internet signals over five miles on public-use radio broadcast frequencies. In 2004, several vendors offered fully secured, encrypted Wi-Fi systems with a broadcast range of 30 miles (Snyder, 2004). This new technology will allow schools to share their broadband access with their communities for a small nominal fee. By providing this broadband service, the relationship between schools and communities will be strengthened, and the integration of computers and the Internet will expand into all facets of the students' lives. The digital divide will be bridged, reinventing teaching and learning.

This technological trend allows for a richer delivery of content and enables a robust interactive environment in the schools.

In the past five years, many states have consented to entire schools functioning via the Internet. By 2003, 16 states had established statewide virtual schools. In addition, 24 states allowed for the creation of cyber charter schools—independent public schools that provide education online (Ansell & Park, 2003). With more than 50,000 public school students in the United States taking some kind of online course, this trend is expected to continue and escalate in the future. Given the rapid growth and improvements in online learning through broadband and the greater access to the Internet through Wi-Fi, it is reasonable to predict that online instruction will emerge as a serious competitor to traditional public schools within the next five years.

III. Teaching, Learning, and the Curriculum

Groupware—file-sharing and instant messaging (IM)—is designed to facilitate online collaboration. Peer-to-peer file sharing has been used by millions of students who have downloaded billions of dollars in music from file-sharing servers. For schools, this type of file sharing would allow teachers to have available a vast resource bank of applications and references. The Schools Interoperability Framework (SIF) is an industry effort consisting of 100 hardware and software companies and school districts to revolutionize the management and accessibility of data within schools, enabling the sharing and interaction of data efficiently, reliably and securely. These types of standards will allow content sharing and collaboration to become a part of the learning environment of the future.

The most popular form of groupware, instant messaging (IM), allows for members of a group to communicate via text messages, whether to individuals or to entire groups. The messages appear immediately on the recipient's computer screen. Other features of IM include whiteboards, video-conferencing, live chats, and directed Web surfing. This technology has been almost ignored by schools, because of the lack of security. By making IM an integral part of the education process, schools will extend their legitimate authority online and, in return, harness the technology to support collaboration, both within the school and beyond. Teaching, learning and the curriculum can be transformed into a constructivist shared learning experience as opposed to traditional teacher-centric and teacher-centered practices.

IV. Assessment and Evaluation

Assessment may be defined as any process used to measure the existing knowledge that a student possesses. This implies that assessment can be a teacher's subjective conclusion based on an observation of student performance, or a three-hour standardized test. Assessment may affect decisions about grades, progression, placement, learning styles, teaching methods, and curriculum. In their endeavor to transform assessment to match the content and design of instruction, some schools are progressing more toward what is known as alternative or authentic assessment. Such tools as performance-based assessment, electronic portfolios, graphic organizers, and student-designed assessments are regarded by many educators as more reflective of new curricular objectives and practices of instruction. Authentic assessment activities require students to apply critical thinking and reasoning to situations such as those they will encounter in the world outside the classroom.

Simultaneously, there are dramatically increased student assessment reporting requirements of both state and the No Child Left Behind act (NCLB). Most schools are required to develop a coherent system of learning outcomes, instruction based on the outcomes, and an assessment system that is aligned with the outcomes and the instruction. The assessments, which must be valid, reliable and fair, are intended to form the basis for making sound decisions about students and instructional programs. How do educators comply with these mandates while effectively and efficiently assessing student skills and learning processes in the classroom?

Schools have begun to invest in the purchase of instructional management systems and assessment software. Used in conjunction with standards-based rubrics to assess authentic learning and performance, these systems meet the criteria for reporting valid and reliable data, while simultaneously offering a clear picture of student progress and needed improvement. The teachers' rubrics serve as scoring guides that differentiate, on a weighted scale, among a group of sample behaviors or evidences of thought that are responding to the same directive. Given the strong national spotlight on student achievement and accountability, educational technology affords a powerful cache of tools to advance student achievement and to create accountability archetypes based on ongoing improvement. To transform teaching and learning to reflect the demands of the 21st century, schools must align assessments to measure the impact of instruction and the contribution of technology to that instruction.

In 2005, a great change occurred in the way districts and states spent and prioritized for educational technology. It was the first year that spending for data management was greater than spending for instructional technology (*Education Week*, 2005). This trend has been spurred by applications in the business community for data-driven decision making and the mandates of NCLB. The ultimate goals are to better target remediation; to identify weaknesses and strengths in particular demographic areas and subjects; and to better address student mobility and transfer between schools—all areas that contribute to educational inequities along racial and socioeconomic lines. It is part of a larger strategy of accountability and the use of educational technology in American education.

V. Productivity and Professional Practice

State-of-the-art technology has become an everyday occurrence. In order to produce technologically proficient and successful students for the current and future hi-tech society, teachers look to technology facilitators and leaders for effective in-service training as well as continual growth in technical knowledge and skills. Technology facilitators and experts must assist teachers in the ongoing development of technology skills, providing assistance in identifying appropriate technology resources aligned with federal and state standards and with state and district technology plans. They must model appropriate strategies for continual learning and establish positive interpersonal relationships with teachers. Technology facilitators and leaders are expected to develop an in-depth understanding of technology operations and concepts in the present, as well as for future potential. With this knowledge, they will in turn impart these skills to other educators to make integration of technology a successful and enjoyable endeavor. The ultimate benefit will be realized by students. Teachers will become technology integration experts.

Ongoing professional development provides opportunities for teachers to expand and improve their teaching skills. Problems that stand in the way of effective technology use include fear of failure and lack of competency; lack of appropriate allotment of time to learn and practice new skills; and fear of increasing workload. Mentoring is one solution to help fearful or novice educators feel more comfortable and become more accomplished incorporating technology in their teaching. A carefully designed and implemented mentoring program can be a highly effective form of professional development. Another remedy is to change the format of one- and two-hour workshops that do not have a great deal of follow-up and practice. Well-designed professional development helps to refresh and extend teacher's subject knowledge, thus maintaining their enthusiasm. Thirdly, administrations need to support their staff by providing time and opportunities for professional development and investing in current technologies.

An important component of the school environment is having personnel within the school assist educators as they navigate through networked systems, educational software, and new techniques that incorporate technology into the classroom. Hiring qualified technology facilitators and leaders who are aware of the standards for productivity and professional practice ensures success.

VI. Social, Ethical, Legal, and Human Issues

The presence of technology in the classroom brings with it new challenges for ensuring responsible use. A host of technology-related issues that schools are facing include privacy, piracy, security, equality, literacy, intellectual property, ethical conduct, and "netiquette"—etiquette in regard to the Internet. Schools and districts are in the process of adopting policies regarding acceptable use of the Internet for students and staff. Technology facilitators and leaders are not only responsible for developing school policies, but also for helping teachers and students grapple with social, ethical, legal, and human issues that arise.

Many schools have developed policies that comply with the federal Children's Internet Protection Act (CIPA), which provides a framework for schools to develop a comprehensive and effective strategy to address these social, ethical, legal and human issues. The legislation requires districts that use E-rate funds to put in place a technology protection measure guarding against students' access to obscene materials, child pornography, and other online content harmful to students. CIPA also requires that districts monitor student use of the Internet and develop an Internet safety system. This system must address such concerns as access to unsuitable materials; the safety and security

Teachers as Technology Leaders

of students when using electronic communications; unauthorized access and other unlawful online actions; and unauthorized disclosure, use, and dissemination of personal information about students.

Digital Rights Management (DRM) refers to the software and hardware used to protect and control access to electronic intellectual property. It is a particularly important topic because it redefines the relationship between copyright and fair use in the digital age. Many fear that the ease and power to track and control the number or times an audio is heard, a video is viewed, or an article is read will squelch legitimate applications of fair use. Both the movie and recording industries and the American Library Association (ALA) plan major educational campaigns with conflicting emphases on copyright and the applications of fair use. Beside the ALA, another response to what is seen as an over-reaching power of copyright holders is a sliding scale of copyright protections. Creative Commons offers copyright holders the ability to offer their material for pubic use under a spectrum of conditions that are less stringent than traditional copyright law.

Teachers need to be aware of the current social, ethical, legal, and human issues that arise with the increasing use of new technologies. Technology facilitators and leaders play a major role in guiding and supporting teachers to understand and enforce technology policies such as copyright, privacy, and netiquette.

VII. Procedures, Policies, Planning, and Budgeting for Technology Environments

By 2003, the rapid growth of school technology infrastructure led to the increased availability and use of computers in schools. Since that time, most students now have access to computers and the Internet in their classrooms, nearly all students have access somewhere in their schools, and a majority of teachers report integrating computers or the Internet into their lessons (Ansell & Park, 2003). Actual budgets for technology in most school districts, however, focus more on the hardware than professional development or technical support. Less than 10% of a typical school district's instructional technology budget is allocated for learning to use and integrate technology. Many educational technology leaders have recommended a more substantial provision for professional development. For this to occur, priorities need to change. As technology in the schools mature, more money should be going to technical support and staff development.

Recently, John Bailey, Director of Educational Technology at the U.S. Department of Education, said that the new Enhancing Education through Technology funding will require that at least 25% be spent on professional development. This program, also called Title II Part D, is key for technology funding under the No Child Left Behind Act (NCLB), signed into law in 2002. It is designed to help schools meet the NCLB Act's goals of improving academic achievement through technology and blending that technology into teacher training and curriculum development. According to the U.S. Department of Education, $700 million in federal formula-based grants have been made available through Title II Part D.

Under the new federal legislation, many programs, including Title I and Reading First, allow expanded funding for education technology. The U.S. government has allocated more than $700 million for implementation of the NCLB, much of it specifically earmarked for educational technology and technology training. Given its scale and influence, NCLB is sure to inspire controversy and debate in the years ahead. Despite its seeming restrictions, the law does help public school districts throughout the country enrich learning by acquiring instructional technologies and funding teacher training (Zielinski, 2004).

Obviously, there will be a continued need for hardware expenses. Antiquated machines will need to be replaced on a regular basis. However, substitution costs should not displace funding for support and development. What good is technology without facilitators to use it effectively? Future trends in planning and budgeting must concentrate on professional development and technology integration.

VIII. Leadership and Vision

District technology leaders have the most influential voice in district technology decisions. To create and sustain a vision for integrating technology into teaching and learning, districts need to create full-time positions for technology leaders. This position should be deeply involved in the district's educational goals and strategies. Investing in technology leadership will foster a strong culture to support more effective integration of technology into the schools.

Millenials, mostly the children of Generation X, are the ones filling the classrooms today. These children are the largest group of young spenders in history, with their parents and grandparents buying their video games, DVDs, and Xboxes. At the same time, their parents have shown the desire to be a part of their children's education, involving themselves in school policy and teaching techniques and decisions. It is not only desired but is expected that the schools support and encourage the technology that the Millenials know and use at home.

Schools and districts have continued to make remarkable progress acquiring hardware, establishing connectivity; ensuring teachers receive technology training and integrating digital content into the curriculum. Technology facilitators and leaders must continue to grow technologically and become agents of change. They should be active in research that supports their technology practices and stay abreast on the new techno-tools and strategies. They should also be willing to utilize their leadership and vision skills and expertise to support decisions for technology integration into classroom instruction. Today's teachers as technology leaders must possess analytical and listening skills, because true leadership and vision involves insight into what will work today, tomorrow, and in the future.

Appendixes

appendix A
Glossary

Advanced Programs. Programs at post-baccalaureate levels for (1) the continuing education of teachers who have previously competed initial preparation or (2) the preparation of *other school professionals.* Advanced programs commonly award graduate credit and include master's, specialist, and doctoral degree programs as well as non-degree licensure programs offered at the post baccalaureate level. Examples of these programs include those for teachers who are preparing for a second license at the graduate level in a field different from the field in which they have their first license; programs for teachers who are seeking a master's degree in the field in which they teach; and programs not tied to licensure, such as programs in curriculum and instruction. In addition, advanced programs include those for other school professionals. Examples of these are programs in school counseling, school psychology, educational administration, and reading specialists (NCATE, proposed 2006).

Assessment System. A comprehensive and integrated set of evaluation measures that provides information for use in monitoring candidate performance and managing and improving unit operations and programs for the preparation of professional educators (NCATE, 2002).

Board of Examiners. On-site evaluators who review institutions based on the NCATE Unit Standards. BOE members are nominated by NCATE-constituent organizations and must successfully complete the NCATE training (NCATE, proposed 2006).

Candidates. Individuals admitted to, or enrolled in, programs for the initial or advanced preparation of teachers, teachers continuing their professional development, or other school personnel. Candidates are distinguished from "students" in P–12 schools (NCATE, 2002).

Conceptual Framework. An underlying structure in a professional education unit that gives conceptual meanings through an articulated rationale to the unit's operation and provides direction for programs, courses, teaching, candidate performance, faculty scholarship and service, and unit accountability (NCATE, 2002).

Data-driven Decision Making (DDDM). A system of teaching and management practices that gets better information about students into the hands of classroom teachers (McLeod, 2005).

Dispositions. See professional dispositions.

Initial Teacher Preparation. Programs at baccalaureate or post-baccalaureate levels that prepare candidates for the first license to teach (NCATE, 2002).

National Educational Technology Standards for Students (NETS•S). The National Educational Technology Standards for Students is designed to provide teachers, technology planners, teacher preparation institutions, and educational decision-makers with frameworks and standards to guide them in establishing enriched learning environments supported by technology.

National Educational Technology Standards for Teachers (NETS•T). The International Society for Technology in Education (ISTE) NETS for Teachers project, a U.S. Department of Education, Preparing Tomorrow's Teachers to Use Technology grant facilitated a series of activities and events resulting in a national consensus on what teachers should know about and be able to do with technology.

Professional Dispositions. The behaviors demonstrated as educators interact with students, families, colleagues and communities, which are expected of professionals and support student learning and development. NCATE expects candidates to demonstrate classroom behaviors that are consistent with the ideas of fairness and the belief that all students can learn. Based on their mission, professional education units may determine additional professional dispositions they want candidates to develop. NCATE expects institutions to assess professional dispositions based on observable behavior in educational settings (NCATE, proposed 2006).

Program. A planned sequence of courses and experiences for the purpose of preparing teachers and other school professionals to work in pre-kindergarten through twelfth grade settings. Programs may lead to a degree, a recommendation for a state license, both, or neither (NCATE, proposed 2006).

Rubrics. Written and shared criteria for judging performance that indicate the qualities by which levels of performance can be differentiated and that anchor judgments about the degree of success on a candidate assessment (NCATE, 2002).

SPAs (Specialized Professional Associations). The national organizations that represent teachers, professional educators, faculty, and other school personnel who teach a specific subject matter (e.g., mathematics or social studies); teach students at a specific developmental level (i.e., early childhood, elementary, middle level, or secondary); teach students with specific needs (e.g., bilingual education or special education); administer schools (e.g., principals or superintendents); or provide services to students (e.g., school counselors or school psychologists). Many of these associations are constitutional members of NCATE and have standards for both students in schools and candidates preparing to work in schools (NCATE, 2002).

SPA Program Review. The process by which the specialized professional associations assess the quality of teacher preparation programs offered by an institution. (Institutions are required to submit their programs for review by SPAs as part of the NCATE preconditions process, unless the state's program standards have been approved by NCATE's Specialty Areas Studies Board for the review of the institutions' teacher education programs (NCATE, 2002).

Students. Children and youth attending P–12 schools as distinguished from teacher candidates (NCATE, 2002).

Unit. The college, school, department, or other administrative body with the responsibility for managing or coordinating all programs offered for the initial and advanced preparation of teachers and other school personnel, regardless of where these programs are administratively housed. Also known as the "professional education unit." The professional education unit must include in its accreditation review all programs offered by the institution for the purpose of preparing teachers and other school professionals to work in pre-kindergarten through twelfth grade settings (NCATE, proposed 2006).

NCATE glossary terms reprinted with permission from the National Council for Accreditation of Teacher Education. All Rights Reserved. At printing, proposed definitions have been approved by the relevant NCATE policy boards and are awaiting ratification by the NCATE Executive Board.

appendix B
References

Ansell, S.E. & Park, J. (2003). Tracking tech trends. *Education Week* 22(35), 43–44, 48.

Barrett, H. (2004). Differentiating electronic portfolios and online assessment management systems. Proceedings of the 2004 Annual Conference of the Society for Information Technology in Teacher Education. Retrieved January 21, 2005 from http://electronicportfolios.org/systems/concerns.html

Cambridge, B., Kahn, S., Tompkins, D., & Yancey, K. (2001). *Electronic portfolios: Emerging practices in student, faculty, and institution learning.* Washington, DC: American Association for Higher Education.

Daggett, W.R. (2005). *Preparing students for their future.* Presentation at June 2005 Model Schools Conference, Nashville, Tennessee, June 26–29, 2005.

Education Week. (2005). *Technology counts 2005.* Retrieved January 3, 2006 from www.edweek.org/ew/toc/2005/05/05/index.html (Registration required).

Educational technology integration program skills set matrix. (1999). Retrieved January 9, 2006 from Pennsylvania State University Web site: https://courses.worldcampus.psu.edu/public/EdTech/programmaterials/SkillsSet.html

Farstrup, A.E. (2004, January 22). *Recommendations of the task force on program review to the NCATE executive board.* Retrieved October 20, 2005 from www.ncate.org/documents/taskforce/taskforceprogramreview.pdf

Frazier, M. & Bailey, G. (2004). *The technology coordinator's handbook.* Eugene, OR: International Society for Technology in Education.

In practice. (2005, May). Blackboard. Retrieved December 11, 2005 from www.blackboard.com/company/newsletters/ASMay2005c.htm

ISTE. (n.d.). Educational computing and technology programs: Technology facilitation initial endorsement. *ISTE NETS Project.* Retrieved October 23, 2005 from http://cnets.iste.org/ncate/n_fac-stands.html

ISTE. (2000). *National educational technology standards for students: Connecting curriculum and technology.* Eugene, OR: International Society for Technology in Education.

ISTE. (2002). *National educational technology standards for teachers: Preparing teachers to use technology.* Eugene, OR: International Society for Technology in Education.

ISTE. (2004a, July 28). *Program report for the preparation of Technology Facilitation teachers.* Retrieved October 14, 2005 from http://cnets.iste.org/ISTENCATE/1bTFWebReport-Aug.doc

ISTE. (2004b). *Technology facilitation rubric.* Retrieved January 13, 2006 from http://cnets.iste.org/ncate/n_fac-rubrics.html

Louisiana State Board of Elementary and Secondary Education. (2001). *Certification criteria educational technology facilitation and educational technology leadership.* [Brochure]. LA: Louisiana Technology Consortium for Teacher Education.

McLeod, S. (2005). *Technology tools for data driven teachers.* Microsoft. Retrieved on November 23, 2005 from www.microsoft.com/Education/ThoughtLeadersDDDM.mspx

Merrow, J. (2001). Undermining standards. *Phi Delta Kappan, 82*(9), 653–665.

NCATE. (n.d.). *NCATE Handbook for Accreditation Visits.* Retrieved January 9, 2006 from www.ncate.org/documents/handbook/handbook.pdf

NCATE. (n.d.). *NCATE's mission.* Retrieved January 9, 2006 from www.ncate.org/documents/NCATEMission.pdf

NCATE. (2001). *NCATE at 50.* Retrieved January 8, 2006 from www.ncate.org/documents/15YearsofGrowth.pdf

NCATE. (2002). *Professional standards: Accreditation of schools, colleges, and departments of education.* Retrieved December 10, 2005 from www.ncate.org/documents/unit_stnds_2002.pdf

NCATE. (2004). *Guidelines for Preparing a Revised Program Report to be Submitted Spring 2006.* Retrieved April 28, 2006 from www.ncate.org/documents/programReview/GuidelinesRevisedProgramReport.doc

NCATE. (2006). *Guidelines and procedures for the NCATE Web-based program review system.* Retrieved December 15, 2005 from www.ncate.org/public/guidelinesProcedures.asp?ch=90

Raths, J. (1999). National Accreditation in Teacher Education: Issues Old and New. University of Delaware. Retrieved April 9, 2006: www.udel.edu/educ/raths/ducharme%20final.htm

Roblyer, M.D. (2003). Then, now & beyond: Getting our NETS worth. *Learning & Leading with Technology, 30*(8).

Salzman, S., Denner, P., & Harris, L. (2002). *Teacher education outcomes measures: Special study survey.* Washington, DC: American Association of Colleges of Teacher Education (ERIC Document Reproduction Services No. ED465791)

Snyder, D.P. (2004, January). A look at the future. *American School Board Journal 191,* 01. Retrieved January 9, 2006 from www.asbj.com/2004/01/0104technologyfocus.html

Vail School District. (2002). *Vail School District job description.* Retrieved December 1, 2005 from Vail School District Web site: www.vail.k12.az.us/employment/jobdescriptions/SiteTechCoord.htm

Visions 2020.2: Student Views on Transforming Education and Training Through Advanced Technologies. (2005). *U.S. Department of Commerce and the U.S. Department of Education NetDay. August* 2005. Retrieved December 23, 2005 from www.netday.org/downloads/Visions2020-2.pdf

WebCT. (2005). *Quality Assessment Innovation Project.* Retrieved December 11, 2005 from www.Webct.com/quality

Wirt, J. et al. (2002). *The Condition of Education 2002.* National Center for Education Statistics, U.S. Department of Education. Washington, DC.

Zielinski, D. (2004). No nickel left behind. *Presentations,* 18(9), 31–34.

Teachers as Technology Leaders

Technology Facilitation and Leadership Scoring Rubrics

Technology Facilitation Scoring Rubrics

Technology Facilitation Standard I. (TF-I)

Technology Operations and Concepts. Educational technology facilitators demonstrate an in-depth understanding of technology operations and concepts. Educational technology facilitators:

Performance Indicator	Approaches Standard	Meets Standard	Exceeds Standard
A. Demonstrate knowledge, skills, and understanding of concepts related to technology (as described in the ISTE National Educational Technology Standards for Teachers). Candidates:			
TF-I.A.1	Make appropriate choices about technology systems, resources, and services that are aligned with district and state standards.	Assist teachers in the ongoing development of knowledge, skills, and understanding of technology systems, resources, and services that are aligned with district and state technology plans.	Conduct needs assessment to determine baseline data on teachers' knowledge, skills, and understanding of concepts related to technology.
TF-I.A.2	Demonstrate an awareness of knowledge and skills related to technology concepts.	Provide assistance to teachers in identifying technology systems, resources, and services to meet specific learning needs.	Evaluate the effectiveness of modeling used to demonstrate teachers' knowledge, skills, and understanding of concepts related to technology.
B. Demonstrate continual growth in technology knowledge and skills to stay abreast of current and emerging technologies. Candidates:			
TF-I.B.1	Identify capabilities and limitations of current and emerging technology resources and assess the potential of these systems and services to address personal, lifelong learning, and workplace needs.	Model appropriate strategies essential to continued growth and development of the understanding of technology operations and concepts.	Evaluate the effectiveness of modeling appropriate strategies essential to continued growth and development of the understanding of technology operations and concepts.

Technology Facilitation Standard II. (TF-II)

Planning and Designing Learning Environments and Experiences. Educational technology facilitators plan, design, and model effective learning environments and multiple experiences supported by technology. Educational technology facilitators:

Performance Indicator	Approaches Standard	Meets Standard	Exceeds Standard
A. Design developmentally appropriate learning opportunities that apply technology-enhanced instructional strategies to support the diverse needs of learners. Candidates:			
TF-II.A.1	Arrange equitable access to appropriate technology resources that enable students to engage successfully in learning activities across subject/content areas and grade levels.	Provide resources and feedback to teachers as they create developmentally appropriate curriculum units that use technology.	Model the creation of developmentally appropriate curriculum units that use technology.
TF-II.A.2	Plan for, implement, and evaluate the management of student use of technology resources to support the diverse needs of learners including adaptive and assistive technologies.	Consult with teachers as they design methods and strategies for teaching computer/ technology concepts and skills within the context of classroom learning.	Model methods and strategies for teaching computer/ technology concepts and skills within the context of classroom learning.
TF-II.A.3	Demonstrate an awareness of technology resources and strategies to support the diverse needs of learners including adaptive and assistive technologies.	Assist teachers as they use technology resources and strategies to support the diverse needs of learners including adaptive and assistive technologies.	Model strategies to support the diverse needs of learners including adaptive and assistive technologies and disseminate information to teachers.
B. Apply current research on teaching and learning with technology when planning learning environments and experiences. Candidates:			
TF-II.B.1	Engage in ongoing planning of lesson sequences that effectively integrate technology resources and are consistent with current best practices for integrating the learning of subject matter and student technology standards.	Assist teachers as they apply current research on teaching and learning with technology when planning learning environments and experiences.	Model strategies reflecting current research on teaching and learning with technology when planning learning environments and experiences.

C. Identify and locate technology resources and evaluate them for accuracy and suitability. Candidates:

TF-II.C.1	Demonstrate an awareness of technology systems, resources, and services that are aligned with district and state standards.	Assist teachers as they identify and locate technology resources and evaluate them for accuracy and suitability based on district and state standards.	Model the use of technology resources reflecting district and state standards.
TF-II.C.2	Make appropriate choices about technology systems, resources, and services that are aligned with district and state standards.	Model technology integration using resources that reflect content standards.	Create professional development lessons integrating technology resources that reflect content standards.

D. Plan for the management of technology resources within the context of learning activities. Candidates:

TF-II.D.1	Engage in ongoing planning of lesson sequences that ensure the management of technology resources within the context of learning activities.	Provide teachers with options for the management of technology resources within the context of learning activities.	Model the use of technology resources within the context of learning activities.

E. Plan strategies to manage student learning in a technology-enhanced environment. Candidates:

TF-II.E.1	Engage in ongoing planning of lesson sequences that manage student learning in a technology-enhanced environment.	Provide teachers with a variety of strategies to use to manage student learning in a technology-enhanced environment and support them as they implement the strategies.	Model a variety of strategies to manage student learning in a technology-enhanced environment and support the teachers as they implement the strategies.

F. Identify and apply instructional design principles associated with the development of technology resources. Candidates:

TF-II.F.1	Plan and implement technology-based learning activities that include an understanding of instructional design principles.	Assist teachers as they identify and apply instructional design principles associated with the development of technology resources.	Model the use of appropriate instructional design principles associated with the development of technology resources.

Technology Facilitation Standard III. (TF-III)

Teaching, Learning, and the Curriculum. Educational technology facilitators apply and implement curriculum plans that include methods and strategies for utilizing technology to maximize student learning. Educational technology facilitators:

Performance Indicator	Approaches Standard	Meets Standard	Exceeds Standard
A. Facilitate technology-enhanced experiences that address content standards and student technology standards. Candidates:			
TF-III.A.1	Demonstrate an awareness of methods and strategies for teaching concepts and skills that support integration of technology productivity tools (refer to NETS for Students).	Use methods and strategies for teaching concepts and skills that support integration of technology productivity tools (refer to NETS for Students).	Analyze methods and facilitate strategies for teaching concepts and skills that support integration of technology productivity tools (refer to NETS for Students).
TF-III.A.2	Demonstrate an awareness of methods and strategies for teaching concepts and skills that support integration of communication tools (refer to NETS for Students).	Use and apply major research findings and trends related to the use of technology in education to support integration throughout the curriculum.	Summarize major research findings and trends related to the use of technology in education to support integration throughout the curriculum.
TF-III.A.3	Demonstrate an awareness of methods and strategies for teaching concepts and skills that support integration of research tools (refer to NETS for Students).	Use methods and strategies for teaching concepts and skills that support integration of research tools (refer to NETS for Students).	Analyze methods and facilitate teachers as they use strategies for teaching concepts and skills that support integration of research tools (refer to NETS for Students).
TF-III.A.4	Demonstrate an awareness of methods and strategies for teaching concepts and skills that support integration of problem-solving/ decision-making tools (refer to NETS for Students).	Use methods and strategies for teaching concepts and skills that support integration of problem-solving/ decision-making tools (refer to NETS for Students).	Analyze methods and facilitate strategies for teaching concepts and skills that support integration of problem-solving/decision-making tools (refer to NETS for Students).
TF-III.A.5	Demonstrate an awareness of methods and strategies for teaching concepts and skills that support use of media-based tools such as television, audio, print media, and graphics.	Use methods and strategies for teaching concepts and skills that support use of media-based tools such as television, audio, print media, and graphics.	Analyze methods and facilitate strategies for teaching concepts and skills that support use of media-based tools such as television, audio, print media, and graphics.

TF-III.A.6	Demonstrate an awareness of methods and strategies for teaching concepts and skills that support use of distance learning systems appropriate in a school environment.	Use and describe methods and strategies for teaching concepts and skills that support use of distance learning systems appropriate in a school environment.	Analyze methods and strategies for teaching concepts and skills that support use of distance learning systems appropriate in a school environment.
TF-III.A.7	Demonstrate an awareness of methods for teaching concepts and skills that support use of Web-based and non Web-based authoring tools in a school environment.	Use methods for teaching concepts and skills that support use of Web-based and non Web-based authoring tools in a school environment.	Analyze methods for teaching concepts and skills that support use of Web-based and non Web-based authoring tools in a school environment.

B. Use technology to support learner-centered strategies that address the diverse needs of students. Candidates:

TF-III.B.1	Demonstrate an awareness of methods and strategies for integrating technology resources that support the needs of diverse learners including adaptive and assistive technology.	Use methods and strategies for integrating technology resources that support the needs of diverse learners including adaptive and assistive technology.	Analyze methods and strategies for integrating technology resources that support the needs of diverse learners including adaptive and assistive technology.

C. Apply technology to demonstrate students' higher-order skills and creativity. Candidates:

TF-III.C.1	Demonstrate an awareness of methods and strategies for teaching problem-solving principles and skills using technology resources.	Use methods and facilitate strategies for teaching problem-solving principles and skills using technology resources.	Analyze methods and facilitate strategies for teaching problem-solving principles and skills using technology resources.

D. Manage student learning activities in a technology-enhanced environment. Candidates:

TF-III.D.1	Develop an awareness of methods and classroom management strategies for teaching technology concepts and skills in individual, small group, classroom, and/or lab settings.	Use methods and classroom management strategies for teaching technology concepts and skills in individual, small group, classroom, and/or lab settings.	Analyze methods and classroom management strategies for teaching technology concepts and skills in individual, small group, classroom, and/or lab settings.

139

E. Use current research and district/region/state/national content and technology standards to build lessons and units of instruction. Candidates:		
TF-III.E.1	Develop an awareness of curricular methods and strategies that are aligned with district/region/state/national content and technology standards.	Describe and identify curricular methods and strategies that are aligned with district/region/state/national content and technology standards.	Disseminate information regarding curricular methods and strategies that are aligned with district/region/state/national content and technology standards.
TF-III.E.2	Develop an awareness of major research findings and trends related to the use of technology in education to support integration throughout the curriculum.	Use major research findings and trends related to the use of technology in education to support integration throughout the curriculum.	Summarize and disseminate major research findings and trends related to the use of technology in education to support integration throughout the curriculum.

Teachers as Technology Leaders

Technology Facilitation Standard IV. (TF-IV)

Assessment and Evaluation. Educational technology facilitators apply technology to facilitate a variety of effective assessment and evaluation strategies. Educational technology facilitators:

Performance Indicator	Approaches Standard	Meets Standard	Exceeds Standard
A. Apply technology in assessing student learning of subject matter using a variety of assessment techniques. Candidates:			
TF-IV.A.1	Develop an awareness of technology tools to collect, analyze, interpret, represent, and communicate data for the purposes of instructional planning and school improvement.	Model the use of technology tools to assess student learning of subject matter using a variety of assessment techniques.	Analyze methods and facilitate the use of strategies to assess student learning of subject matter using a variety of assessment techniques.
TF-IV.A.2	Use results from assessment measures to improve instructional planning, management, and implementation of learning strategies.	Assist teachers in using technology to improve learning and instruction through the evaluation and assessment of artifacts and data.	Analyze methods and facilitate the use of strategies to improve learning and instruction through the evaluation and assessment of artifacts and data.
B. Use technology resources to collect and analyze data, interpret results, and communicate findings to improve instructional practice and maximize student learning. Candidates:			
TF-IV.B.1	Implement a variety of instructional technology strategies and grouping strategies that include appropriate embedded assessment for meeting the diverse needs of learners.	Guide teachers as they use technology resources to collect and analyze data, interpret results, and communicate findings to improve instructional practice and maximize student learning.	Examine the validity and reliability of technology resources to collect and analyze data, interpret results, and communicate findings to improve instructional practice and maximize student learning.
C. Apply multiple methods of evaluation to determine students' appropriate use of technology resources for learning, communication, and productivity. Candidates:			
TF-IV.C.1	Guide students in applying self- and peer-assessment tools to critique student-created technology products and the process used to create the products.	Assist teachers in using recommended evaluation strategies for improving students' use of technology resources for learning, communication, and productivity.	Recommend evaluation strategies for improving students' use of technology resources for learning, communication, and productivity.

Technology Facilitation Standard V. (TF-V)

Productivity and Professional Practice. Educational technology facilitators apply technology to enhance and improve personal productivity and professional practice. Educational technology facilitators:

Performance Indicator	Approaches Standard	Meets Standard	Exceeds Standard
A. Use technology resources to engage in ongoing professional development and lifelong learning. Candidates:			
TF-V.A.1	Participate in professional development activities and professional technology organizations to support ongoing professional growth related to technology.	Identify resources and participate in professional development activities and professional technology organizations to support ongoing professional growth related to technology.	Use resources and professional development activities available from professional technology organizations to support ongoing professional growth related to technology.
TF-V.A.2	Develop an awareness of district-wide policies for the professional growth opportunities for staff, faculty, and administrators.	Disseminate information on district-wide policies for professional growth opportunities for staff, faculty, and administrators.	Implement policies that support district-wide professional growth opportunities for staff, faculty, and administrators.
B. Continually evaluate and reflect on professional practice to make informed decisions regarding the use of technology in support of student learning. Candidates:			
TF-V.B.1	Reflect on professional practice to make informed decisions regarding the use of technology in support of student learning.	Continually evaluate and reflect on professional practice to make informed decisions regarding the use of technology in support of student learning.	Continually evaluate professional practice to make informed decisions regarding the use of technology in support of student learning and disseminate findings to district administrators.
C. Apply technology to increase productivity. Candidates:			
TF-V.C.1	Model features of word processing, desktop publishing, graphics programs, and utilities to demonstrate professional products.	Model advanced features of word processing, desktop publishing, graphics programs, and utilities to develop professional products.	Model the integration of advanced features of word processing, desktop publishing, graphics programs, and utilities to demonstrate professional products.

Teachers as Technology Leaders

TF-V.C.2	Locate, select, capture, and integrate video and digital images, in varying formats for use in presentations, publications and/or other products.	Assist others in locating, selecting, capturing, and integrating video and digital images, in varying formats for use in presentations, publications, and/or other products.	Facilitate activities to help others in locating, selecting, capturing, and integrating video and digital images, in varying formats for use in presentations, publications and/or other products.
TF-V.C.3	Use specific-purpose electronic devices (such as graphing calculators, languages translators, scientific probeware, or electronic thesaurus) in content areas.	Demonstrate the use of specific-purpose electronic devices (such as graphing calculators, language translators, scientific probeware, or electronic thesaurus) in content areas.	Facilitate the use of specific-purpose electronic devices (such as graphing calculators, languages translators, scientific probeware, or electronic thesaurus) in content areas.
TF-V.C.4	Develop an awareness of several distance-learning systems to support personal/ professional development.	Use a variety of distance learning systems and use at least one to support personal and professional development.	Use a variety of distance learning systems to support personal/professional development.
TF-V.C.5	Develop an awareness of instructional design principles and its importance in the development of hypermedia and multimedia products.	Use instructional design principles to develop hypermedia and multimedia products to support personal and professional development.	Apply instructional design principles to demonstrate hypermedia/multimedia products to support professional development.
TF-V.C.6	Describe appropriate tools for communicating concepts, conducting research, and solving problems for an intended audience and purpose.	Select appropriate tools for communicating concepts, conducting research, and solving problems for an intended audience and purpose.	Model the use of appropriate tools for communicating concepts, conducting research, and solving problems for an intended audience and purpose.
TF-V.C.7	Develop an awareness of examples of emerging programming, authoring or problem-solving environments that support personal/professional development.	Use examples of emerging programming, authoring, or problem-solving environments that support personal and professional development.	Use examples of emerging programming, authoring or problem-solving environments that support personal/professional development.

TF-V.C.8	Identify preferences and defaults of operating systems and productivity tool programs that can be set to support personal and professional development.	Set and manipulate preferences, defaults and other selectable features of operating systems and productivity tool programs commonly found in P–12 schools.	Set and manipulate preferences and defaults of operating systems and productivity tool programs, and troubleshoot problems associated with their operation.
D. Use technology to communicate and collaborate with peers, parents, and the larger community in order to nurture student learning. Candidates:			
TF-V.D.1	Use telecommunications tools and resources for information sharing, remote information access, and multimedia/hypermedia publishing in order to nurture student learning.	Model the use of telecommunications tools and resources for information sharing, remote information access, and multimedia/hypermedia publishing in order to nurture student learning.	Stay abreast of current telecommunications tools and resources for information sharing, remote information access, and multimedia/hypermedia publishing in order to nurture student learning.
TF-V.D.2	Communicate with colleagues about current research to support instruction, using electronic mail and Web browsers.	Communicate with colleagues and discuss current research to support instruction, using applications including electronic mail, online conferencing and Web browsers.	Communicate with colleagues and apply current research to support instruction, using applications including electronic mail, online conferencing and Web browsers.
TF-V.D.3	Participate in online collaborative curricular projects and team activities.	Participate in online collaborative curricular projects and team activities to build bodies of knowledge around specific topics.	Investigate and disseminate online collaborative curricular projects and team activities to build bodies of knowledge around specific topics.
TF-V.D.4	Design, demonstrate and maintain Web pages and sites that support personal productivity.	Design and maintain Web pages and sites that support communication between the school and community.	Design, maintain, and facilitate the development of Web pages and sites that support communication between teachers, school, and community.

Technology Facilitation Standard VI. (TF-VI)

Social, Ethical, Legal, and Human Issues. Educational technology facilitators understand the social, ethical, legal, and human issues surrounding the use of technology in P–12 schools and assist teachers in applying that understanding in their practice. Educational technology facilitators:

Performance Indicator	Approaches Standard	Meets Standard	Exceeds Standard
A. Model and teach legal and ethical practice related to technology use. Candidates:			
TF-VI.A.1	Demonstrate and advocate legal and ethical behaviors among students, colleagues, and community members regarding the use of technology and information.	Develop strategies and provide professional development at the school/classroom level for teaching social, ethical, and legal issues and responsible use of technology.	Analyze rules, policies, and procedures to support the legal and ethical use of technology.
TF-VI.A.2	Summarize copyright laws related to use of images, music, video, and other digital resources in varying formats.	Assist others in summarizing copyright laws related to use of images, music, video, and other digital resources in varying formats.	Plan activities that focus on copyright laws related to use of images, music, video, and other digital resources in varying formats.
B. Apply technology resources to enable and empower learners with diverse backgrounds, characteristics, and abilities. Candidates:			
TF-VI.B.1	Facilitate students' use of technology that addresses their social needs and cultural identity and promotes their interaction with the global community.	Assist teachers in selecting and applying appropriate technology resources to enable and empower learners with diverse backgrounds, characteristics, and abilities.	Analyze and recommend appropriate technology resources to enable and empower learners with diverse backgrounds, characteristics, and abilities.
TF-VI.B.2	Facilitate students' use of technology that addresses their special needs.	Identify, classify and recommend adaptive/assistive hardware and software for students and teachers with special needs and assist in procurement and implementation.	Analyze and recommend appropriate adaptive/assistive hardware and software for students and teachers with special needs and assist in procurement and implementation.

C. Identify and use technology resources that affirm diversity. Candidates:			
TF-VI.C.1	Identify capabilities and limitations of current and emerging technology resources that affirm diversity.	Assist teachers in selecting and applying appropriate technology resources to affirm diversity and address cultural and languages differences.	Recommend appropriate technology resources to affirm diversity and address cultural and language differences.

D. Promote safe and healthy use of technology resources. Candidates:			
TF-VI.D.1	Enforce classroom procedures that guide students' safe and healthy use of technology and that comply with legal and professional responsibilities.	Assist teachers in selecting and applying appropriate technology resources to promote safe and healthy use of technology.	Recommend appropriate technology resources to promote safe and healthy use of technology.

E. Facilitate equitable access to technology resources for all students. Candidates:			
TF-VI.E.1	Advocate equal access to technology for all students and teachers.	Develop a summary of effective school policies and classroom management strategies for achieving equitable access to technology resources for all students and teachers.	Conduct research to determine effective strategies for achieving equitable access to technology resources for all students and teachers.

Technology Facilitation Standard VII. (TF-VII)

Procedures, Policies, Planning, and Budgeting for Technology Environments. Educational technology facilitators promote the development and implementation of technology infrastructure, procedures, policies, plans, and budgets for P–12 schools. Educational technology facilitators:

Performance Indicator	Approaches Standard	Meets Standard	Exceeds Standard
A. Use the school technology facilities and resources to implement classroom instruction. Candidates:			
TF-VII.A.1	Identify plans to configure computer/technology systems and related peripherals in laboratory, classroom cluster, and other appropriate instructional arrangements.	Use plans to configure software/computer/technology systems and related peripherals in laboratory, classroom cluster, and other appropriate instructional arrangements.	Stay abreast of current developments to configure computer/technology systems and related peripherals in laboratory, classroom cluster, and other appropriate instructional arrangements.
TF-VII.A.2	Identify local mass storage devices and media to store and retrieve information and resources.	Use local mass storage devices and media to store and retrieve information and resources.	Stay abreast of local mass storage devices and media to store and retrieve information and resources.
TF-VII.A.3	Identify issues related to selecting, installing, and maintaining wide area networks (WAN) for school districts.	Discuss issues related to selecting, installing, and maintaining wide area networks (WAN) for school districts.	Differentiate among issues related to selecting, installing, and maintaining wide area networks (WAN) for school districts, and facilitate integration of technology infrastructure with the WAN.
TF-VII.A.4	Use software in classroom and administrative settings including productivity tools, information access/telecommunication tools, multimedia/hypermedia tools, school management tools, evaluation/portfolio tools, and computer-based instruction.	Model integration of software used in classroom and administrative settings including productivity tools, information access/telecommunication tools, multimedia/hypermedia tools, school management tools, evaluation/portfolio tools, and computer-based instruction.	Analyze software used in classroom and administrative settings including productivity tools, information access/telecommunication tools, multimedia/hypermedia tools, school management tools, evaluation/portfolio tools, and computer-based instruction.
TF-VII.A.5	Identify methods of installation, maintenance, inventory, and management of software libraries.	Utilize methods of installation, maintenance, inventory, and management of software libraries.	Analyze and critique methods of installation, maintenance, inventory, and management of software libraries.

TF-VII.A.6	Develop an awareness of strategies for troubleshooting and maintaining various hardware/software configurations found in school settings.	Use and apply strategies for troubleshooting and maintaining various hardware/software configurations found in school settings.	Stay abreast of current strategies for troubleshooting and maintaining various hardware/software configurations found in school settings.
TF-VII.A.7	Develop an awareness of network software packages used to operate a computer network system.	Utilize network software packages used to operate a computer network system.	Evaluate network software packages used to operate a computer network system and/or local area network (LAN).
TF-VII.A.8	Develop an awareness of the important roles for technology support personnel to assume to empower teachers and students to maximize technology resources to enhance student learning.	Work with technology support personnel to maximize the use of technology resources by administrators, teachers, and students to improve student learning.	Identify areas where support personnel are needed to manage and enhance use of technology resources in the school by administrators, teachers and students.
B. Follow procedures and guidelines used in planning and purchasing technology resources. Candidates:			
TF-VII.B.1	Develop an awareness of instructional software to support and enhance the school curriculum and demonstrate recommendations for purchase.	Identify instructional software to support and enhance the school curriculum and develop recommendations for purchase.	Evaluate instructional software to support and enhance the school curriculum and demonstrate recommendations for purchase.
TF-VII.B.2	Develop an awareness of guidelines for budget planning and management procedures related to educational computing and technology facilities and resources.	Discuss and apply guidelines for budget planning and management procedures related to educational computing and technology facilities and resources.	Analyze guidelines for budget planning and management procedures related to educational computing and technology facilities and resources.
TF-VII.B.3	Develop an awareness of procedures related to troubleshooting and preventive maintenance on technology infrastructure.	Discuss and apply procedures related to troubleshooting and preventive maintenance on technology infrastructure.	Stay abreast of current procedures related to troubleshooting and preventive maintenance on technology infrastructure.

TF-VII.B.4	Develop an awareness of current information involving facilities planning issues and computer-related technologies.	Apply current information involving facilities planning issues and computer-related technologies.	Analyze and apply current information involving facilities planning issues and computer-related technologies.
TF-VII.B.5	Develop an awareness of policies and procedures concerning staging, scheduling, and security for managing computers/technology in a variety of school/laboratory/classroom settings.	Suggest policies and procedures concerning staging, scheduling, and security for managing computers/technology in a variety of school/laboratory/classroom settings.	Apply policies and procedures concerning staging, scheduling, and security for managing computers/technology in a variety of school/laboratory/classroom settings.
TF-VII.B.6	Develop an awareness of distance learning facilities.	Use distance and online learning facilities.	Use distance and online learning facilities routinely.
TF-VII.B.7	Develop an awareness of recommended specifications for purchasing technology systems in school settings.	Describe and identify recommended specifications for purchasing technology systems in school settings.	Research specifications for purchasing technology systems.

C. **Participate in professional development opportunities related to management of school facilities, technology resources, and purchases. Candidates:**

TF-VII.C.1	Identify opportunities for technology professional development at the building/school level utilizing adult learning theory.	Support technology professional development at the building/school level utilizing adult learning theory.	Design and plan technology professional development at the building/school level utilizing adult learning theory.

Teachers as Technology Leaders

Technology Facilitation Standard VIII. (TF-VIII)

Leadership and Vision. Educational technology facilitators will contribute to the shared vision for campus integration of technology and foster an environment and culture conducive to the realization of the vision. Educational technology facilitators:

Performance Indicator	Approaches Standard	Meets Standard	Exceeds Standard
A. Utilize school technology facilities and resources to implement classroom instruction. Candidates:			
TF-VIII.A.1	Develop an awareness of current research in educational technology.	Discuss and evaluate current research in educational technology.	Locate and disseminate current research in educational technology.
B. Apply strategies for and knowledge of issues related to managing the change process in schools. Candidates:			
TF-VIII.B.1	Develop an awareness of the history of technology use in schools.	Discuss the history of technology use in schools.	Develop and implement activities that focus on the history of technology use in schools.
C. Apply effective group process skills. Candidates:			
TF-VIII.C.1	Develop an awareness of the importance of forming school partnerships to support technology integration and examine an existing partnership within a school setting.	Discuss the rationale for forming school partnerships to support technology integration and examine an existing partnership within a school setting.	Provide information on the benefits of forming school partnerships to support technology integration and locate an existing partnership within a school setting.
D. Lead in the development and evaluation of district technology planning and implementation. Candidates:			
TF-VIII.D.1	Develop an awareness of the importance of using cooperative group processes.	Participate in cooperative group processes and identify the processes that were effective.	Disseminate information on effective cooperative group processes.
TF-VIII.D.2	Develop an awareness of the importance of the school technology environment.	Conduct an evaluation of a school technology environment.	Create an evaluation instrument to use to conduct an evaluation of a school technology environment.
TF-VIII.D.3	Recognize the importance of national, state, and local standards for integrating technology in the school environment.	Identify and discuss national, state, and local standards for integrating technology in the school environment.	Examine the impact of national, state, and local standards for integrating technology in the school environment.

TF-VIII.D.4	Examine curriculum activities or performances that meet national, state, and local technology standards.	Describe curriculum activities or performances that meet national, state, and local technology standards.	Examine the impact of curriculum activities or performances that meet national, state, and local technology standards.
TF-VIII.D.5	Develop an awareness of the issues related to developing a school technology plan.	Discuss issues related to developing a school technology plan.	Determine essential components of a school technology plan.
TF-VIII.D.6	Develop an awareness of the issues related to hardware and software acquisition and management.	Examine issues related to hardware and software acquisition and management.	Determine strategies and procedures needed for resource acquisition and management of technology-based systems including hardware and software.
E. Engage in supervised field-based experiences with accomplished technology facilitators and/or directors. Candidates:			
TF-VIII.E.1	Develop an awareness of the components needed for effective field-based experiences in instructional program development, professional development, facility and resource management, WAN/LAN/wireless systems, or managing change related to technology use in school-based settings.	Examine components needed for effective field-based experiences in instructional program development, professional development, facility and resource management, WAN/LAN/wireless systems, or managing change related to technology use in school-based settings.	Determine components needed for effective field-based experiences in instructional program development, professional development, facility and resource management, WAN/LAN/wireless systems, or managing change related to technology use in school-based settings.

Technology Leadership Scoring Rubrics

Technology Leadership Standard I. (TL-I)

Technology Operations and Concepts. Educational technology leaders demonstrate an in-depth understanding of technology operations and concepts. Educational technology leaders:

Performance Indicator	Approaches Standard	Meets Standard	Exceeds Standard
A. Demonstrate knowledge, skills, and understanding of conepts related to technology (as described in the ISTE National Educational Technology Standards for Teachers). Candidates:			
TL-I.A.1	Conduct needs assessment to determine baseline data on teachers' knowledge, skills, and understanding of concepts related to technology.	Identify and evaluate components needed for the continual growth of knowledge, skills, and understanding of concepts related to technology.	Develop and implement a professional development model that ensures continual growth in knowledge, skills, and understanding of concepts related to technology.
TL-I.A.2	Evaluate the effectiveness of modeling used to develop teachers' knowledge, skills, and understanding of concepts related to technology.	Offer a variety of professional development opportunities that facilitate the ongoing development of knowledge, skills, and understanding of concepts related to technology.	Assess a variety of professional development opportunities that facilitate the ongoing development of knowledge, skills, and understanding of concepts related to technology.
B. Demonstrate continual growth in technology knowledge and skills to stay abreast of current and emerging technologies. Candidates:			
TL-I.B.1	Evaluate the effectiveness of the modeling of appropriate strategies essential to continued growth and development of the understanding of technology operations and concepts.	Offer a variety of professional development opportunities that facilitate the continued growth and development of the understanding of technology operations and concepts.	Develop and assess a variety of professional development opportunities that facilitate the continued growth and development of the understanding of technology operations and concepts.

Technology Leadership Standard II. (TL-II)

Planning and Designing Learning Environments and Experiences. Educational technology leaders plan, design, and model effective learning environments and multiple experiences supported by technology. Educational technology leaders:

Performance Indicator	Approaches Standard	Meets Standard	Exceeds Standard
A. Design developmentally appropriate learning opportunities that apply technology-enhanced instructional strategies to support the diverse needs of learners. Candidates:			
TL-II.A.1	Model the creation of developmentally appropriate curriculum units that use technology.	Research and disseminate project-based instructional units modeling appropriate uses of technology to support learning.	Build an online database of project-based instructional units modeling appropriate uses of technology to support learning.
TL-II.A.2	Model methods and strategies for teaching computer/technology concepts and skills within the context of classroom learning.	Identify and evaluate methods and strategies for teaching computer/technology concepts and skills within the context of classroom learning and coordinate dissemination of best practices at the district/state/regional level.	Identify and evaluate methods and strategies for teaching computer/technology concepts and skills within the context of classroom learning and coordinate dissemination of best practices at the national and international level.
TL-II.A.3	Model strategies to support the diverse needs of learners including adaptive and assistive technologies and disseminate information to teachers.	Stay abreast of current technology resources and strategies to support the diverse needs of learners including adaptive and assistive technologies and disseminate information to teachers.	Develop technology resources and strategies to support the diverse needs of learners including adaptive and assistive technologies and disseminate information to teachers.
B. Apply current research on teaching and learning with technology when planning learning environments and experiences. Candidates:			
TL-II.B.1	Model strategies reflecting current research on teaching and learning with technology when planning learning environments and experiences.	Locate and evaluate current research on teaching and learning with technology when planning learning environments and experiences.	Conduct research on teaching and learning with technology when planning learning environments and experiences.

153

C. Identify and locate technology resources and evaluate them for accuracy and suitability. Candidates:

TL-II.C.1	Model the use of technology resources reflecting district and state standards.	Identify technology resources and evaluate them for accuracy and suitability based on the content standards.	Develop technology resources based on the content standards.
TL-II.C.2	Create professional development activities that reflect content standards and integrate technology resources.	Provide ongoing appropriate professional development to disseminate the use of technology resources that reflect content standards.	Develop, implement, and assess a professional development model aligning technology resources and content standards.

D. Plan for the management of technology resources within the context of learning activities. Candidates:

TL-II.D.1	Model the use of technology resources within the context of learning activities.	Identify and evaluate options for the management of technology resources within the context of learning activities.	Research findings on the management of technology resources within the context of learning activities and create a professional development model.

E. Plan strategies to manage student learning in a technology-enhanced environment. Candidates:

TL-II.E.1	Model a variety of strategies to manage student learning in a technology-enhanced environment and support the teachers as they implement the strategies.	Continually evaluate a variety of strategies to manage student learning in a technology-enhanced environment and disseminate through professional development activities.	Conduct research on a variety of strategies to manage student learning in a technology-enhanced environment and disseminate results.

F. Identify and apply instructional design principles associated with the development of technology resources. Candidates:

TL-II.F.1	Model the use of appropriate instructional design principles associated with the development of technology resources.	Identify and evaluate instructional design principles associated with the development of technology resources.	Develop, implement and evaluate a professional development model for assisting teachers in the identification and application of instructional design principles associated with the development of technology resources.

Technology Leadership Standard III. (TL-III)

Teaching, Learning, and the Curriculum. Educational technology leaders apply and implement curriculum plans that include methods and strategies for applying technology to maximize student learning. Educational technology leaders:

Performance Indicator	Approaches Standard	Meets Standard	Exceeds Standard
A. Facilitate technology-enhanced experiences that address content standards and student technology standards. Candidates:			
TL-III.A.1	Analyze methods and facilitate strategies for teaching concepts and skills that support integration of technology productivity tools (refer to NETS for students).	Design methods and strategies for teaching concepts and skills that support integration of technology productivity tools (refer to NETS for students).	Model strategies for teaching concepts and skills that support integration of technology productivity tools (refer to NETS for students).
TL-III.A.2	Summarize major research findings and trends related to the use of technology in education to support integration throughout the curriculum.	Design methods for teaching concepts and skills that support integration of communication tools (refer to NETS for students).	Model strategies for teaching concepts and skills that support integration of communication tools (refer to NETS for students).
TL-III.A.3	Analyze methods and support teachers as they use strategies for teaching concepts and skills that support integration of research tools (refer to NETS for students).	Design methods and strategies for teaching concepts and skills that support integration of research tools (refer to NETS for students).	Model strategies for teaching concepts and skills that support integration of research tools (refer to NETS for students).
TL-III.A.4	Analyze methods and facilitate strategies for teaching concepts and skills that support integration of problem-solving/decision-making tools (refer to NETS for students).	Design methods and model strategies for teaching concepts and skills that support integration of problem-solving/decision-making tools (refer to NETS for students).	Implement methods and strategies for teaching concepts and skills that support integration of problem-solving/decision-making tools (refer to NETS for students).
TL-III.A.5	Analyze methods and facilitate strategies for teaching concepts and skills that support use of media-based tools such as television, audio, print media, and graphics.	Design methods and model strategies for teaching concepts and skills that support use of media-based tools such as television, audio, print media, and graphics.	Implement methods and model strategies for teaching concepts and skills that support use of media-based tools such as television, audio, print media, and graphics.

TL-III.A.6	Analyze methods and strategies for teaching concepts and skills that support use of distance learning systems appropriate in a school environment.	Evaluate methods and strategies for teaching concepts and skills that support use of distance learning systems appropriate in a school environment.	Implement methods and strategies for teaching concepts and skills that support use of distance learning systems appropriate in a school environment.
TL-III.A.7	Analyze methods for teaching concepts and skills that support use of Web-based and non Web-based authoring tools in a school environment.	Design methods and model strategies for teaching concepts and skills that support use of Web-based and non Web-based authoring tools in a school environment.	Implement methods and strategies for teaching concepts and skills that support use of Web-based and non Web-based authoring tools in a school environment.

B. Use technology to support learner-centered strategies that address the diverse needs of students. Candidates:

TL-III.B.1	Analyze methods and strategies for integrating technology resources that support the needs of diverse learners including adaptive and assistive technology.	Design methods and strategies for integrating technology resources that support the needs of diverse learners including adaptive and assistive technology.	Implement methods and strategies for integrating technology resources that support the needs of diverse learners including adaptive and assistive technology.

C. Apply technology to demonstrate students' higher-order skills and creativity. Candidates:

TL-III.C.1	Analyze methods and facilitate strategies for teaching problem-solving principles and skills using technology resources.	Design methods and model strategies for teaching hypermedia development, scripting, and/or computer programming, in a problem-solving context in the school environment.	Implement strategies for teaching hyper-media development, scripting, and/or computer programming, in a problem-solving context in the school environment.

D. Manage student learning activities in a technology-enhanced environment. Candidates:

TL-III.D.1	Analyze methods and classroom management strategies for teaching technology concepts and skills in individual, small group, classroom, and/or lab settings.	Design methods and model classroom management strategies for teaching technology concepts and skills used in P–12 environments.	Implement methods and classroom management strategies for teaching technology concepts and skills used in P–12 environments.

E.	Use current research and district/region/state/national content and technology standards to build lessons and units of instruction. Candidates:		
TL-III.E.1	Disseminate information regarding curricular methods and strategies that are aligned with district/region/state/national content and technology standards.	Disseminate curricular methods and strategies that are aligned with district/region/state/national content and technology standards.	Model curricular methods and strategies that are aligned with district/region/state/national content and technology standards.
TL-III.E.2	Summarize and disseminate major research findings and trends related to the use of technology in education to support integration throughout the curriculum.	Investigate major research findings and trends related to the use of technology in education to support integration throughout the curriculum.	Disseminate major research findings and trends related to the use of technology in education to support integration throughout the curriculum.

Teachers as Technology Leaders

Technology Leadership Standard IV. (TL-IV)

Assessment and Evaluation. Educational technology leaders communicate research on the use of technology to implement effective assessment and evaluation strategies. Educational technology leaders:

Performance Indicator	Approaches Standard	Meets Standard	Exceeds Standard
A. Apply technology in assessing student learning of subject matter using a variety of assessment techniques. Candidates:			
TL-IV.A.1	Analyze methods and facilitate the use of strategies to assess student learning of subject matter using a variety of assessment techniques.	Facilitate the development of a variety of techniques to use technology to assess student learning of subject matter.	Develop, implement and assess innovative techniques, which include the use of technology for assessing student learning.
TL-IV.A.2	Analyze methods and facilitate the use of strategies to improve learning and instruction through the evaluation and assessment of artifacts and data.	Provide technology resources for assessment and evaluation of artifacts and data.	Develop, implement and assess innovative technology resources for assessment and evaluation of artifacts and data.
B. Use technology resources to collect and analyze data, interpret results, and communicate findings to improve instructional practice and maximize student learning. Candidates:			
TL-IV.B.1	Examine the validity and reliability of technology resources to collect and analyze data, interpret results, and communicate findings to improve instructional practice and maximize student learning.	Identify and procure technology resources to aid in analysis and interpretation of data.	Develop, implement and assess innovative technology resources to aid in analysis and interpretation of data.
C. Apply multiple methods of evaluation to determine students' appropriate use of technology resources for learning, communication, and productivity. Candidates:			
TL-IV.C.1	Recommend evaluation strategies for improving students' use of technology resources for learning, communication, and productivity.	Design strategies and methods for evaluating the effectiveness of technology resources for learning, communication, and productivity.	Research and disseminate findings on the effectiveness of technology resources for evaluating learning, communication, and productivity.

TL-IV.C.2	Analyze data from a research project that includes evaluating the use of a specific technology in a P–12 environment.	Conduct a research project that includes evaluating the use of a specific technology in a P–12 environment.	Design a research project that includes evaluating the use of several technology resources in a P–12 environment.

Technology Leadership Standard V. (TL-V)

Productivity and Professional Practice. Educational technology leaders design, develop, evaluate and model products created using technology resources to improve and enhance their productivity and professional practice. Educational technology leaders:

Performance Indicator	Approaches Standard	Meets Standard	Exceeds Standard
A. Use technology resources to engage in ongoing professional development and lifelong learning. Candidates:			
TL-V.A.1	Use resources and professional development activities available from professional technology organizations to support ongoing professional growth related to technology.	Design, prepare, and conduct professional development activities to present at the school/district level and at professional technology conferences to support ongoing professional growth related to technology.	Evaluate professional development activities presented at professional technology conferences to support ongoing professional growth related to technology.
TL-V.A.2	Implement policies that support district-wide professional growth opportunities for staff, faculty, and administrators.	Plan and implement policies that support district-wide professional growth opportunities for staff, faculty, and administrators.	Plan, implement, and revise policies that support district-wide professional growth opportunities for staff, faculty, and administrators.
B. Continually evaluate and reflect on professional practice to make informed decisions regarding the use of technology in support of student learning. Candidates:			
TL-V.B.1	Continually evaluate professional practice to make informed decisions regarding the use of technology in support of student learning and disseminate findings to district administrators.	Based on evaluations, make recommendations for changes in professional practices regarding the use of technology in support of student learning.	Implement changes based on recommendations for changes in professional practices regarding use of technology in support of student learning.
C. Apply technology to increase productivity. Candidates:			
TL-V.C.1	Model the integration of advanced features of word processing, desktop publishing, graphics programs, and utilities to develop professional products.	Model the integration of data from multiple software applications using advanced features of applications such as word processing, database, spreadsheet, communication, and other tools into a product.	Create multimedia presentations integrated with multiple types of data using advanced features of a presentation tool and model them to audiences inside and outside the district using computer projection systems.

Teachers as Technology Leaders

TL-V.C.2	Facilitate activities to help others in locating, selecting, capturing, and integrating video and digital images, in varying formats for use in presentations, publications and/or other products.	Create multimedia presentations integrated with multiple types of data using advanced features of a presentation tool and model them to district staff using computer projection systems.	Create multimedia presentations integrated with multiple types of data using advanced features of a presentation tool and model them to audiences inside and outside the district using computer projection systems.
TL-V.C.3	Facilitate the use of specific-purpose electronic devices (such as graphing calculators, language translators, scientific probeware, or electronic thesaurus) in content areas.	Document and assess field-based experiences and observations using specific-purpose electronic devices.	Document and assess field-based experiences and observations using specific-purpose electronic devices and then collaborate with peers regarding results.
TL-V.C.4	Use a variety of distance learning systems to support personal/professional development.	Use distance learning delivery systems to conduct and provide professional development opportunities for students, teachers, administrators, and staff.	Use distance learning delivery systems to conduct and provide professional development opportunities for students, teachers, administrators, and staff and other schools in surrounding communities.
TL-V.C.5	Apply instructional design principles to develop hypermedia/multimedia products to support professional development.	Apply instructional design principles to develop and analyze substantive interactive multimedia computer-based instructional products.	Apply instructional design principles to develop, analyze, and then compare substantive interactive multimedia computer-based instructional products.
TL-V.C.6	Model the use of appropriate tools for communicating concepts, conducting research, and solving problems for an intended audience and purpose.	Design and practice strategies for testing functions and evaluating technology use effectiveness of instructional products that were developed using multiple technology tools.	Design and practice strategies for analyzing content accuracy, testing functions, and evaluating technology use effectiveness of instructional products that were developed using multiple technology tools.

161

TL-V.C.7	Use examples of emerging program-ming, authoring or problem-solving envi-ronments that support personal/professional development.	Analyze examples of emerging programming, authoring or problem-solving environments that support personal and professional development, and make recommendations for integration at school/district level.	Analyze and model examples of emerging programming, authoring or problem-solving envi-ronments that support personal/professional development, and make recommendations for integration at school/district level.
TL-V.C.8	Set and manipulate preferences and defaults of operating systems and produc-tivity tool programs, and troubleshoot problems associated with their operation.	Analyze and modify the features and preferences of major operating systems and/or productivity tool programs when devel-oping products to solve problems encountered with their operation and/or to enhance their capability.	Analyze, evaluate, and modify the features and preferences of major operating systems and/or productivity tool programs when devel-oping products to solve problems encountered with their operation and/or to enhance their capability.
D. Use technology to communicate and collaborate with peers, parents, and the larger community in order to nurture student learning. Candidates:			
TL-V.D.1	Stay abreast of current telecommunications tools and resources for information sharing, remote information access, and multi-media/hypermedia publishing in order to nurture student learning.	Model and implement the use of telecom-munications tools and resources to foster and support informa-tion sharing, remote information access, and communication between students, school staff, parents, and local community.	Model and analyze the use of telecom-munications tools and resources to foster and support informa-tion sharing, remote information access, and communication between students, school staff, parents, and the local/state/national/international community.
TL-V.D.2	Communicate with colleagues and apply current research to support instruction, using applications including electronic mail, online confer-encing and Web browsers.	Organize, coordinate, and participate in an online learning community related to the use of technology to support learning.	Organize, coordinate, and monitor an online learning community designed for students, staff and members of the community related to a predefined curricular subject.

Teachers as Technology Leaders

TL-V.D.3	Investigate and disseminate online collaborative curricular projects and team activities to build bodies of knowledge around specific topics.	Organize and coordinate online collaborative curricular projects with corresponding team activities/responsibilities to build bodies of knowledge around specific topics.	Organize, coordinate, and monitor online collaborative curricular projects with corresponding team activities/responsibilities to build bodies of knowledge around specific topics.
TL-V.D.4	Design, maintain, and facilitate the development of Web pages and sites that support communication between teachers, school, and community.	Design, modify, maintain, and facilitate the development of Web pages and sites that support communication and information access between the entire school district and local/state/national/international communities.	Develop, organize, and conduct professional development to enable site/department Web personnel to develop and modify school-based Web sites.

Technology Leadership Standard VI. (TL-VI)

Social, Ethical, Legal, and Human Issues. Educational technology leaders understand the social, ethical, legal, and human issues surrounding the use of technology in P–12 schools and develop programs facilitating application of that understanding in practice throughout their district/region/state. Educational technology leaders:

Performance Indicator	Approaches Standard	Meets Standard	Exceeds Standard
A. Model and teach legal and ethical practice related to technology use. Candidates:			
TL-VI.A.1	Analyze rules, policies, and procedures to support the legal and ethical use of technology.	Establish and communicate clear rules, policies, and procedures to support legal and ethical use of technologies at the district/region/state levels.	Advocate rules, policies, and procedures to support legal and ethical use of technologies at the national and international level.
TL-VI.A.2	Plan activities that focus on copyright laws related to use of images, music, video, and other digital resources in varying formats.	Implement a plan for documenting adherence to copyright laws.	Implement an evaluation system to determine adherence to copyright laws.
B. Apply technology resources to enable and empower learners with diverse backgrounds, characteristics, and abilities. Candidates:			
TL-VI.B.1	Analyze and recommend appropriate technology resources to enable and empower learners with diverse backgrounds, characteristics, and abilities.	Communicate research on best practices related to applying appropriate technology resources to enable and empower learners with diverse backgrounds, characteristics, and abilities.	Research best practices related to applying appropriate technology resources to enable and empower learners with diverse backgrounds, characteristics, and abilities.
TL-VI.B.2	Analyze and recommend appropriate adaptive/assistive hardware and software for students and teachers with special needs and assist in procurement and implementation.	Develop policies and provide professional development related to acquisition and use of appropriate adaptive/assistive hardware and software for students and teachers with special needs.	Research adaptive/assistive hardware and software for students and teachers with special needs and advocate appropriate use at the national and international level.

C. Identify and use technology resources that affirm diversity. Candidates:			
TL-VI.C.1	Recommend appropriate technology resources to affirm diversity and address cultural and language differences.	Communicate research on best practices related to applying appropriate technology resources to affirm diversity and address cultural and language differences.	Conduct research to determine best practices for applying appropriate technology resources to affirm diversity and address cultural and language differences.

D. Promote safe and healthy use of technology resources. Candidates:			
TL-VI.D.1	Recommend appropriate technology resources to promote safe and healthy use of technology.	Communicate research and establish policies to promote safe and healthy use of technology.	Conduct research and advocate safe and healthy use of technology.

E. Facilitate equitable access to technology resources for all students. Candidates:			
TL-VI.E.1	Conduct research to determine effective strategies for achieving equitable access to technology resources for all students and teachers.	Use research findings in establishing policy and implementation strategies to promote equitable access to technology resources for students and teachers.	Advocate national and international policies that provide equitable access to technology resources for all students and teachers.

Technology Leadership Standard VII. (TL-VII)

Procedures, Policies, Planning, and Budgeting for Technology Environments. Educational technology leaders coordinate development and direct implementation of technology infrastructure procedures, policies, plans, and budgets for P-12 schools. Educational technology leaders:

Performance Indicator	Approaches Standard	Meets Standard	Exceeds Standard
A. Use the school technology facilities and resources to implement classroom instruction. Candidates:			
TL-VII.A.1	Stay abreast of current developments to configure computer/technology systems and related peripherals in laboratory, classroom cluster, and other appropriate instructional arrangements.	Develop plans to configure software/computer/technology systems and related peripherals in laboratory, classroom cluster, and other appropriate instructional arrangements.	Disseminate plans to configure computer/technology systems and related peripherals in laboratory, classroom cluster, and other appropriate instructional arrangements.
TL-VII.A.2	Stay abreast of local mass storage devices and media to store and retrieve information and resources.	Install local mass storage devices and media to store and retrieve information and resources.	Configure local mass storage devices and media to store and retrieve information and resources.
TL-VII.A.3	Differentiate among issues related to selecting, installing, and maintaining wide area networks (WAN) for school districts, and facilitate integration of technology infrastructure with the WAN.	Prioritize issues related to selecting, installing, and maintaining wide area networks (WAN) for school districts, and facilitate integration of technology infrastructure with the WAN.	Make modifications based upon prioritized issues related to selecting, installing, and maintaining wide area networks (WAN) for school districts, and facilitate integration of technology infrastructure with the WAN.
TL-VII.A.4	Analyze software used in classroom and administrative settings including productivity tools, information access/telecommunication tools, multimedia/hypermedia tools, school management tools, evaluation/portfolio tools, and computer-based instruction.	Manage software used in classroom and administrative settings including productivity tools, information access/telecommunication tools, multimedia/hypermedia tools, school management tools, evaluation/portfolio tools, and computer-based instruction.	Evaluate and recommend software used in classroom and administrative settings including productivity tools, information access/telecommunication tools, multimedia/hypermedia tools, school management tools, evaluation/portfolio tools, and computer-based instruction.

TL-VII.A.5	Analyze and critique methods of installation, maintenance, inventory, and management of software libraries.	Evaluate methods of installation, main-tenance, inventory, and management of software libraries.	Implement methods of installation, main-tenance, inventory, and management of software libraries.
TL-VII.A.6	Stay abreast of current strategies for troubleshooting and maintaining various hardware/software configurations found in school settings.	Develop and dissemi-nate strategies for troubleshooting and maintaining various hardware/software configurations found in school settings.	Implement strategies for troubleshooting and maintaining various hardware/software configurations found in school settings.
TL-VII.A.7	Evaluate network software packages used to operate a computer network system and/or local area network (LAN).	Select network software packages used to operate a computer network system and/or local area network (LAN).	Install and maintain network software packages used to operate a computer network system and/or local area network (LAN).
TL-VII.A.8	Identify areas where support personnel are needed to manage and enhance use of technology resources in the school by admin-istrators, teachers and students.	Analyze needs for technology support personnel to manage school/district tech-nology resources and maximize use by admin-istrators, teachers, and students to improve student learning.	Formulate a plan to acquire technology support personnel to manage school/district technology resources and maximize use by administrators, teachers, and students to improve student learning.

B. Follow procedures and guidelines used in planning and purchasing technology resources. Candidates:

TL-VII.B.1	Evaluate instructional software to support and enhance the school curriculum and develop recommendations for purchase.	Investigate purchasing strategies and proce-dures for acquiring administrative and instructional software for educational settings.	Recommend purchasing strategies and proce-dures for acquiring administrative and instructional software for educational settings.
TL-VII.B.2	Analyze guidelines for budget planning and management procedures related to educational computing and technology facili-ties and resources.	Develop and utilize guidelines for budget planning and manage-ment procedures related to educational computing and tech-nology facilities and resources.	Implement guidelines for budget planning and management procedures related to educational computing and technology facili-ties and resources.

Teachers as Technology Leaders

TL-VII.B.3	Stay abreast of current procedures related to troubleshooting and preventive maintenance on technology infrastructure.	Develop and disseminate a system for analyzing and implementing procedures related to troubleshooting and preventive maintenance on technology infrastructure.	Operate a system for analyzing and implementing procedures related to troubleshooting, and preventive maintenance on technology infrastructure.
TL-VII.B.4	Analyze and apply current information involving facilities planning issues and computer-related technologies.	Maintain and disseminate current information involving facilities planning issues and computer-related technologies.	Evaluate current information involving facilities planning issues and computer-related technologies.
TL-VII.B.5	Apply policies and procedures concerning staging, scheduling, and security for managing computers/ technology in a variety of school/laboratory/ classroom settings.	Design and develop policies and procedures concerning staging, scheduling, and security for managing hardware, software, and related technologies in a variety of instructional and administrative school settings.	Evaluate policies and procedures concerning staging, scheduling, and security for managing hardware, software, and related technologies in a variety of instructional and administrative school settings.
TL-VII.B.6	Select distance and online learning facilities and resources.	Research and recommend systems and processes for implementation of distance and online learning facilities and infrastructure.	Operate systems and processes for implementation of distance and online learning facilities and infrastructure.
TL-VII.B.7	Research specifications for purchasing technology systems.	Differentiate among specifications for purchasing technology systems in school settings.	Make recommendations regarding specifications for purchasing technology systems.
C. Participate in professional development opportunities related to management of school facilities, technology resources, and purchases. Candidates:			
TL-VII.C.1	Design and plan technology professional development at the building/school level utilizing adult learning theory.	Implement technology professional development at the school/district level utilizing adult learning theory.	Evaluate technology professional development at the school/district level utilizing adult learning theory.

Teachers as Technology Leaders

Technology Leadership Standard VIII. (TL-VII)

Leadership and Vision. Educational technology leaders will facilitate development of a shared vision for comprehensive integration of technology and foster an environment and culture conducive to the realization of the vision. Educational technology leaders:

Performance Indicator	Approaches Standard	Meets Standard	Exceeds Standard
A. Identify and apply educational and technology-related research, the psychology of learning, and instructional design principles in guiding the use of computers and technology in education. Candidates:			
TL-VIII.A.1	Locate and disseminate current research in educational technology.	Communicate and apply principles and practices of educational research in educational technology.	Conduct research in educational technology.
B. Apply strategies for and knowledge of issues related to managing the change process in schools. Candidates:			
TL-VIII.B.1	Develop and implement activities that focus on the history of technology use in schools.	Describe social and historical foundations of education and how they relate to the use of technology in schools.	Research the social historical foundations of education and how they relate to the use of technology in schools.
C. Apply effective group process skills. Candidates:			
TL-VIII.C.1	Provide information on the benefits of forming school partnerships to support technology integration and locate an existing partnership within a school setting.	Discuss issues relating to building collaborations, alliances, and partnerships involving educational technology initiatives.	Build collaborations, alliances, and partnerships involving educational technology initiatives.
D. Lead in the development and evaluation of district technology planning and implementation. Candidates:			
TL-VIII.D.1	Disseminate information on effective cooperative group processes.	Design and lead in the implementation of an effective group process related to technology leadership or planning.	Use effective group process related to technology leadership or planning.
TL-VIII.D.2	Create an evaluation instrument to use to conduct an evaluation of a school technology environment.	Use evaluation findings to recommend modifications in technology implementations.	Conduct evaluations to determine needed modifications in technology implementations.

Teachers as Technology Leaders

TL-VIII.D.3	Examine the impact of national, state, and local standards for integrating technology in the school environment.	Use national, state, and local standards to develop curriculum plans for integrating technology in the school environment.	Assist in the development of national, state, and local standards for the development of curriculum plans for integrating technology in the school environment.
TL-VIII.D.4	Examine the impact of curriculum activities or performances that meet national, state, and local technology standards.	Develop curriculum activities or performances that meet national, state, and local technology standards.	Assist in the development of national, state, and local standards for the development of curriculum activities or performances.
TL-VIII.D.5	Determine essential components of a school technology plan.	Compare and evaluate district-level technology plans.	Facilitate the development of technology plans.
TL-VIII.D.6	Determine essential elements and strategies for developing a technology strategic plan.	Use strategic planning principles to lead and assist in the acquisition, implementation, and maintenance of technology resources.	Develop strategic planning principles to lead and assist in the acquisition, implementation, and maintenance of technology resources.
TL-VIII.D.7	Determine strategies and procedures needed for resource acquisition and management of technology-based systems including hardware and software.	Plan, develop, and implement strategies and procedures for resource acquisition and management of technology-based systems including hardware and software.	Research to determine effectiveness of strategies and procedures for resource acquisition and management of technology-based systems including hardware and software.
E. Engage in supervised field-based experiences with accomplished technology facilitators and/or directors. Candidates:			
TL-VIII.E.1	Determine components needed for effective field-based experiences in instructional program development, professional development, facility and resource management, WAN/LAN/wireless systems, or managing change related to technology use in school-based settings.	Participate in a significant field-based activity involving experiences in instructional program development, professional development, facility and resource management, WAN/LAN/wireless systems, or managing change related to technology use in school-based settings.	Mentor participants involved in a significant field-based activity involving experiences in instructional program development, professional development, facility and resource management, WAN/LAN/wireless systems, or managing change related to technology use in school-based settings.

National Educational Technology Standards

National Educational Technology Standards for Students (NETS•S)

The National Educational Technology Standards for Students are divided into six broad categories. Standards within each category are to be introduced, reinforced, and mastered by students. Teachers can use these standards as guidelines for planning technology-based activities in which students achieve success in learning, communication, and life skills.

1. **Basic operations and concepts**

   ■ Students demonstrate a sound understanding of the nature and operation of technology systems.

   ■ Students are proficient in the use of technology.

2. **Social, ethical, and human issues**

   ■ Students understand the ethical, cultural, and societal issues related to technology.

   ■ Students practice responsible use of technology systems, information, and software.

   ■ Students develop positive attitudes toward technology uses that support lifelong learning, collaboration, personal pursuits, and productivity.

3. **Technology productivity tools**

   ■ Students use technology tools to enhance learning, increase productivity, and promote creativity.

   ■ Students use productivity tools to collaborate in constructing technology-enhanced models, preparing publications, and producing other creative works.

4. **Technology communications tools**

   ■ Students use telecommunications to collaborate, publish, and interact with peers, experts, and other audiences.

- Students use a variety of media and formats to communicate information and ideas effectively to multiple audiences.

5. **Technology research tools**

   - Students use technology to locate, evaluate, and collect information from a variety of sources.

   - Students use technology tools to process data and report results.

   - Students evaluate and select new information resources and technological innovations based on the appropriateness to specific tasks.

6. **Technology problem-solving and decision-making tools**

   - Students use technology resources for solving problems and making informed decisions.

   - Students employ technology in the development of strategies for solving problems in the real world.

National Educational Technology Standards for Teachers (NETS•T)

All classroom teachers should be prepared to meet the following standards and performance indicators.

I. Technology Operations and Concepts

Teachers demonstrate a sound understanding of technology operations and concepts. Teachers:

   A. demonstrate introductory knowledge, skills, and understanding of concepts related to technology (as described in the ISTE National Educational Technology Standards for Students).

   B. demonstrate continual growth in technology knowledge and skills to stay abreast of current and emerging technologies.

II. Planning and Designing Learning Environments and Experiences

Teachers plan and design effective learning environments and experiences supported by technology. Teachers:

   A. design developmentally appropriate learning opportunities that apply technology-enhanced instructional strategies to support the diverse needs of learners.

   B. apply current research on teaching and learning with technology when planning learning environments and experiences.

Teachers as Technology Leaders

   C. identify and locate technology resources and evaluate them for accuracy and suitability.

   D. plan for the management of technology resources within the context of learning activities.

   E. plan strategies to manage student learning in a technology-enhanced environment.

III. Teaching, Learning, and the Curriculum

Teachers implement curriculum plans that include methods and strategies for applying technology to maximize student learning. Teachers:

   A. facilitate technology-enhanced experiences that address content standards and student technology standards.

   B. use technology to support learner-centered strategies that address the diverse needs of students.

   C. apply technology to develop students' higher-order skills and creativity.

   D. manage student learning activities in a technology-enhanced environment.

IV. Assessment and Evaluation

Teachers apply technology to facilitate a variety of effective assessment and evaluation strategies. Teachers:

   A. apply technology in assessing student learning of subject matter using a variety of assessment techniques.

   B. use technology resources to collect and analyze data, interpret results, and communicate findings to improve instructional practice and maximize student learning.

   C. apply multiple methods of evaluation to determine students' appropriate use of technology resources for learning, communication, and productivity.

V. Productivity and Professional Practice

Teachers use technology to enhance their productivity and professional practice. Teachers:

   A. use technology resources to engage in ongoing professional development and lifelong learning.

   B. continually evaluate and reflect on professional practice to make informed decisions regarding the use of technology in support of student learning.

   C. apply technology to increase productivity.

   D. use technology to communicate and collaborate with peers, parents, and the larger community in order to nurture student learning.

VI. Social, Ethical, Legal, and Human Issues

Teachers understand the social, ethical, legal, and human issues surrounding the use of technology in PK–12 schools and apply that understanding in practice. Teachers:

A. model and teach legal and ethical practice related to technology use.

B. apply technology resources to enable and empower learners with diverse backgrounds, characteristics, and abilities.

C. identify and use technology resources that affirm diversity.

D. promote safe and healthy use of technology resources.

E. facilitate equitable access to technology resources for all students.

National Educational Technology Standards for Administrators (NETS•A)

All school administrators should be prepared to meet the following standards and performance indicators. These standards are a national consensus among educational stakeholders regarding what best indicates effective school leadership for comprehensive and appropriate use of technology in schools.

I. Leadership and Vision—Educational leaders inspire a shared vision for comprehensive integration of technology and foster an environment and culture conducive to the realization of that vision. Educational leaders:

A. facilitate the shared development by all stakeholders of a vision for technology use and widely communicate that vision.

B. maintain an inclusive and cohesive process to develop, implement, and monitor a dynamic, long-range, and systemic technology plan to achieve the vision.

C. foster and nurture a culture of responsible risk taking and advocate policies promoting continuous innovation with technology.

D. use data in making leadership decisions.

E. advocate research-based effective practices in use of technology.

F. advocate, on the state and national levels, policies, programs, and funding opportunities that support implementation of the district technology plan.

II. Learning and Teaching—Educational leaders ensure that curricular design, instructional strategies, and learning environments integrate appropriate technologies to maximize learning and teaching. Educational leaders:

A. identify, use, evaluate, and promote appropriate technologies to enhance and support instruction and standards-based curriculum leading to high levels of student achievement.

B. facilitate and support collaborative technology-enriched learning environments conducive to innovation for improved learning.

C. provide for learner-centered environments that use technology to meet the individual and diverse needs of learners.

D. facilitate the use of technologies to support and enhance instructional methods that develop higher-level thinking, decision-making, and problem-solving skills.

E. provide for and ensure that faculty and staff take advantage of quality professional learning opportunities for improved learning and teaching with technology.

III. Productivity and Professional Practice—Educational leaders apply technology to enhance their professional practice and to increase their own productivity and that of others. Educational leaders:

A. model the routine, intentional, and effective use of technology.

B. employ technology for communication and collaboration among colleagues, staff, parents, students, and the larger community.

C. create and participate in learning communities that stimulate, nurture, and support faculty and staff in using technology for improved productivity.

D. engage in sustained, job-related professional learning using technology resources.

E. maintain awareness of emerging technologies and their potential uses in education.

F. use technology to advance organizational improvement.

IV. Support, Management, and Operations—Educational leaders ensure the integration of technology to support productive systems for learning and administration. Educational leaders:

A. develop, implement, and monitor policies and guidelines to ensure compatibility of technologies.

B. implement and use integrated technology-based management and operations systems.

C. allocate financial and human resources to ensure complete and sustained implementation of the technology plan.

D. integrate strategic plans, technology plans, and other improvement plans and policies to align efforts and leverage resources.

E. implement procedures to drive continuous improvements of technology systems and to support technology-replacement cycles.

V. **Assessment and Evaluation—Educational leaders use technology to plan and implement comprehensive systems of effective assessment and evaluation. Educational leaders:**

   A. use multiple methods to assess and evaluate appropriate uses of technology resources for learning, communication, and productivity.

   B. use technology to collect and analyze data, interpret results, and communicate findings to improve instructional practice and student learning.

   C. assess staff knowledge, skills, and performance in using technology and use results to facilitate quality professional development and to inform personnel decisions.

   D. use technology to assess, evaluate, and manage administrative and operational systems.

VI. **Social, Legal, and Ethical Issues—Educational leaders understand the social, legal, and ethical issues related to technology and model responsible decision making related to these issues. Educational leaders:**

   A. ensure equity of access to technology resources that enable and empower all learners and educators.

   B. identify, communicate, model, and enforce social, legal, and ethical practices to promote responsible use of technology.

   C. promote and enforce privacy, security, and online safety related to the use of technology.

   D. promote and enforce environmentally safe and healthy practices in the use of technology.

   E. participate in the development of policies that clearly enforce copyright law and assign ownership of intellectual property developed with district resources.

This material was originally produced as a project of the Technology Standards for School Administrators Collaborative.

Teachers as Technology Leaders